Mary Green Carroll
from ?

Love to Mary Agnes
from Bird.

Christmas 1955

GOD
LOVE
YOU

Books by Bishop Sheen

GOD AND INTELLIGENCE
RELIGION WITHOUT GOD
THE LIFE OF ALL LIVING
THE DIVINE ROMANCE
OLD ERRORS AND NEW LABELS
MOODS AND TRUTHS
THE WAY OF THE CROSS
THE SEVEN LAST WORDS
THE ETERNAL GALILEAN
THE PHILOSOPHY OF SCIENCE
THE MYSTICAL BODY OF CHRIST
CALVARY AND THE MASS
THE MORAL UNIVERSE
THE CROSS AND THE BEATITUDES
THE CROSS AND THE CRISIS
LIBERTY, EQUALITY AND FRATERNITY
THE RAINBOW OF SORROW
VICTORY OVER VICE
WHENCE COME WARS
THE SEVEN VIRTUES
FOR GOD AND COUNTRY
A DECLARATION OF DEPENDENCE
GOD AND WAR
THE DIVINE VERDICT
THE ARMOR OF GOD
PHILOSOPHIES AT WAR
SEVEN WORDS TO THE CROSS
SEVEN PILLARS OF PEACE
LOVE ONE ANOTHER
FREEDOM UNDER GOD
COMMUNISM AND THE CONSCIENCE OF THE WEST
THE PHILOSOPHY OF RELIGION
PEACE OF SOUL
LIFT UP YOUR HEART
THREE TO GET MARRIED
THE WORLD'S FIRST LOVE
LIFE IS WORTH LIVING
WAY TO HAPPINESS
LIFE IS WORTH LIVING: SERIES TWO
WAY TO INNER PEACE
GOD LOVE YOU

GOD

LOVE

YOU

MOST REVEREND FULTON J. SHEEN, PH.D., D.D.

AGRÉGÉ EN PHILOSOPHIE DE L'UNIVERSITÉ DE LOUVAIN. AUXIL-
IARY BISHOP OF NEW YORK. NATIONAL DIRECTOR, WORLD MISSION
SOCIETY FOR THE PROPAGATION OF THE FAITH

GARDEN CITY BOOKS
GARDEN CITY, NEW YORK

Dedicated
to
The Blessed Virgin Mary
Who
Gave Human Life
to
Divine Life
In the Person of Her Son, Jesus Christ,
Who
in His Turn,
Gave His Life,
in Love for Us

ACKNOWLEDGMENTS

The author and Garden City Books wish to thank the following publishers for their kind permission to use selections from works by the author as listed below.

MCGRAW-HILL BOOK COMPANY, INC.: *Peace of Soul.* Copyright, 1949, by Fulton J. Sheen. *Lift up Your Heart.* Copyright, 1950, by Fulton J. Sheen. *The World's First Love.* Copyright, 1952, by Fulton J. Sheen.

APPLETON-CENTURY-CROFTS, INC.: *Three to Get Married.* Copyright, 1951, by Fulton J. Sheen. *The Divine Romance.* Copyright, 1930, by The Century Company. *Moods and Truths.* Copyright, 1932, by The Century Company. *Old Errors and New Labels.* Copyright, 1931, by The Century Company. *The Eternal Galilean.* Copyright, 1934, by D. Appleton-Century, Inc. *The Life of All Living.* Copyright, 1929, by The Century Company. *The Seven Last Words.* Copyright, 1933, by The Century Company.

P. J. KENEDY & SONS: *The Armor of God,* copyright, 1943, P. J. Kenedy & Sons, New York. *For God and Country,* copyright, 1941, P. J. Kenedy & Sons. *The Cross and the Beatitudes,* copyright, 1937, P. J. Kenedy & Sons. *Love One Another,* copyright, 1944, P. J. Kenedy & Sons. *Calvary and the Mass,* copyright, 1936, P. J. Kenedy & Sons. *Victory over Vice,* copyright, 1939, P. J. Kenedy & Sons. *Seven Words of Jesus and Mary,* copyright, 1945, P. J. Kenedy & Sons. *Characters of the Passion,* copyright, 1947, P. J. Kenedy & Sons. *Preface to Religion,* copyright, 1946, P. J. Kenedy & Sons. *The Seven Virtues,* copyright, 1940, P. J. Kenedy & Sons. *Seven Words to the Cross,* copyright, 1944, P. J. Kenedy & Sons. *The Rainbow of Sorrow,* copyright, 1938, P. J. Kenedy & Sons. *God and War,* copyright, 1942, P. J. Kenedy & Sons.

THE GEORGE MATTHEW ADAMS SERVICE: *Way to Inner Peace,* copyright, 1949, 1950, 1951, 1952, 1953, 1954, by The George Matthew Adams Service, and copyright, 1954, by Maco Magazine Corporation. *Way to Happiness,* copyright, 1949, 1950, 1951, 1952, 1953, by The George Matthew Adams Service, and copyright, 1953, by Maco Magazine Corporation.

LONGMANS, GREEN & COMPANY: *Religion without God,* copyright, 1928, by Longmans, Green & Company.

THE BOBBS-MERRILL COMPANY, INC.: *Communism and the Conscience of the West,* copyright, 1948, by Fulton J. Sheen.

GOD
LOVE
YOU

J

O Y is the happiness of love—love aware of its own inner happiness. Pleasure comes from without, but joy comes from within, and it is, therefore, within the reach of everyone in the world. For if there is sadness in our hearts, it is because there is not enough love. But to be loved, we must be lovable; to be lovable, we must be good; to be good, we must know Goodness; and to know Goodness, is to love God, and neighbor, and everybody in the world.

  L o v e that desires to limit its own exercise is not love. Love that is happier if it meets only one who needs help than if it met ten, and happiest if it met none at all, is not love. One of love's essential laws is expressed in the words of Our Lord that the Apostles fondly remembered after He ascended: "It is more blessed to give than to receive." Our nation will be happier and our hearts will be gayer when we discover the true brotherhood of man, but to do this we must realize that we are

11

a race of illegitimate children unless there is also the Father-hood of God.

❧ OUR Divine Lord was interested in studying the alms-givers and it was the quality of their giving which arrested Him, far more than the quantity they gave. He had once said that where our treasure is, there our heart is, also. Now He tells us that where the heart goes, there the treasure follows. Few of us have His attitude towards alms; we do not trouble to read the list of donors in fine type under the heading, *"Amounts less than . . ."* But probably that would be to Him the most important section of the list; on that occasion in the temple He immortalized a gift of two of the smallest coins in the ancient world.

❧ WE BEGIN to act differently when we recognize the immensity of our possibilities. Our whole life changes then, like that of a farmer when he discovers oil on what he had previously believed to be just a poor farm. Prayer overcomes sadness by putting us in relation with the Eternal, and then the change occurs. Before, we had thought ourselves unloved by anyone; now, we know that we are loved by God.

❧ HERE is a psychological suggestion for acquiring peace of soul. Never brag; never talk about yourself; never rush to first seats at table or in a theater; never use people for your own advantage; never lord it over others as if you were better than they.

These are but popular ways of expressing the virtue of humility, which does not consist so much in humbling ourselves before others as it does in recognizing our own littleness in comparison to what we ought to be.

❧ IN THE face of Divine Wisdom, all that we have, or do, or know, is a gift of God, and is only an insignificant molehill compared to His Mountain of Knowledge. Well indeed then may those who enjoy any relative superiority ask with Paul: "What have you that you have not received? If so, then why glory as if you had not received."

⋙ OUR LIVES for the most part are made up of little things, and by these our character is to be tested. There are very few who have to take a prominent place in the great conflicts of our age; the vast majority must dwell in humbler scenes and be content to do a more humble work. The conflicts which a man has to endure either against evil in his own soul or in the moral circle where his influence would seem to be trivial are in reality the struggle of the battle for life and decency; and true heroism is shown here as well as in those grander scales in which others win the leader's fame or the martyr's crown. Little duties carefully discharged; little temptations earnestly resisted with the strength which God supplies; little sins crucified; these all together help to form that character which is to be described not as popular or glamorous, but as moral and noble.

⋙ MAN IS much more inclined to concentrate his moral actions in one great moment and thereby often wins the merits of a hero. The woman, on the contrary, scatters her tiny little sacrifices through life and multiplies them to such an extent that very few give her the credit for sacrifice because it has been so multiplied.

⋙ THERE is a world of difference between submitting to the Divine Will from sullenness and submitting to it knowing that God is Supreme Wisdom, and that some day we will know all that happened, happened for the best. There is a marvelous peace that comes into the soul if all trials and disappointments, sorrows and pains are accepted either as a deserved chastisement for our sins, or as a healthful discipline which will lead us to greater virtue. The violin strings, if they were conscious, would complain when the musician tightened them, but this is because they do not see that the sacrificial strain was necessary before they could produce a perfect melody. Evils actually become lighter by patient endurance and benefits are poisoned by discontent.

⋖§ INNER PEACE can be won only by making God the ruler of *all* that we do. Many people who believe in God refuse to go this far: they keep Him in a small compartment of their minds. Their plans are laid without consulting Him; their trials and sufferings are endured with no recollection of the fact that Love may hurt in order to cure; their days are passed in loneliness and weariness, although each hour might have been filled with sweetness.

To such hearts a single moment of grace may work the change. They suddenly become aware that "the Lord is in the house." Better still: the Lord is in our hearts. They are no longer self-centered, now, but they are God-centered; outer events of their lives can no longer ruffle their peace.

⋖§ BY THE Divine standard, true greatness is indicated neither by the possession of great abilities nor the buzz of popular applause. Any talent a person has, such as a talent for singing, speaking, or writing, is a gift of God. He has done nothing more to merit it than a child with a beautiful face. "If then, thou has received, why dost thou glory, as if thou hadst not received." The richer the gifts, the greater the responsibilities on the day of Judgment.

⋖§ IF WE are to do good to others, they must be loved for God's sake. No moral profit comes from doing good to another because "he can get it for us wholesale" or from giving gifts to others because of the pleasure they give us. There is not even great merit in doing good to those who love us. "You love those who love you. Do not the heathens this?" The greatest spiritual profit comes from loving those who hate us, and from giving gifts and dinners to those who cannot give anything in return, for then recompense will be made in the Kingdom of Heaven.

&⸲ T H E R E are two ways of knowing how good God is. One is never to lose Him; the other is to lose Him and find Him again.

&⸲ P E R H A P S no one understands us better than saints, not only because they correct their bad judgment of us through their own weakness, but also because they see us as souls precious in the sight of God. St. Francis de Sales used to say: "O the beautiful souls of sinners." It was not their sins he loved, but their souls. The Curé of Ars used to walk two or three blocks alongside his country Church where there was a long line of penitents waiting to see him. He would pick out the great sinners and reserve for them the greatest sympathy. When one is in trouble, one should never go for advice to one who never says prayers or who has not passed through suffering.

&⸲ T w o considerations are helpful in developing a good disposition. The first is to be mindful that a happy conscience makes a happy outlook on life, and an unhappy conscience makes us miserable on the inside and everyone else miserable on the outside. When our conscience bothers us, whether we admit it or not, we often try to justify it by correcting others, or by finding fault with them. The readiness to believe evil about others is in a large part ammunition for a thousand scandals in our own hearts. But by finding black spots in others, they believe they distract attention from their own miserable state. The good conscience, on the contrary, finds good in others even when there is some discontent with self.

&⸲ T H E secret of growing old is in this counsel an old man once gave a youth: "Repent on your last day." But the youth answered: "But who knows when is my last day?" For that reason said the Saint: "Repent today for it would be tomorrow."

✥ TOLERANCE is not right when its basic principle is a denial of truth and goodness and when it asserts that it makes no difference whether murder is a blessing or a crime, or whether a child should be taught to steal or to respect the rights of others.

But there can be another form of tolerance which is right, such as one inspired by true charity or love of God. Even though a virtuous man may hold absolutely to his philosophy of life, he does so, not because he looks down on the views of others as not as good as his own, but because his own beliefs are so real to him that he would not have anyone else hold them with less reason, less love and less devotion.

✥ IN SILENCE, there is humility of spirit or what might be called a "wise passiveness." In such the ear is more important than the tongue. God speaks, but not in cyclones— only in the zephyrs and gentle breezes. As the scientist learns by sitting passively before nature, so the soul learns wisdom by being responsive to His Will. The scientist does not tell nature its laws; nature tells the scientist. Man does not tell or impose his will on God; in silence like Mary, he awaits an Annunciation.

✥ WHEN we judge others, we also judge ourselves. Our Lord asked us not to judge, lest we be judged; and sometimes the judgment we make of others is in itself a condemnation of our own faults. When one woman calls another "catty," she reveals that she knows what cattiness involves. Jealousy can be a tribute paid by mediocrity to genius: the jealous person then admits the superiority of his rival but since he cannot reach that level himself, he drags the other down to his. Other forms of criticism are equally revealing of the one who criticizes.

16

◈ T H E bitterest draught man can ever drink is the confession of his utter inadequacy. The world says that at this moment man is at his worst; actually he is at his best. Man is at his worst if he falls into despair; but he is at his best if humbled he cries to God for help.

◈ A S S O C I E T Y is made by man, so man, in his turn, is made by his thoughts, his decisions and his choices. Nothing ever happens to the world which did not first happen inside the mind of some man: the material of the skyscraper merely completes the architect's dream. Even the material of our physical selves is the servant of our thoughts: psychologists recognize the fact that our bodies may become tired only because of tiredness in the mind. Worry, anxiety, fear and boredom are felt as physical: mind-fatigue appears to us as bodily fatigue.

◈ O U R H A P P I N E S S consists in fulfilling the purpose of our being. Every man knows, from his own unfulfilled hunger for them, that he was built with a capacity for three things of which he never has enough. He wants life—not for the next few minutes, but for always, and with no aging or disease to threaten it. He also wants to grasp truth—not with a forced choice between the truths of mathematics or geography, but he wants all truth. Thirdly, he wants love—not with a time-limit, not mixed with satiety or disillusionment, but love that will be an abiding ecstasy.

These three things are not to be found in this life in their completion: on earth life is shadowed by death, truth mingles with error, love is mixed with hate. But men know they would not long for these things in their purity if there were no possibility of ever finding them. So, being reasonable, they search for the source from which these mixed and imperfect portions of life, love, truth derive.

◈ I N L O O K I N G for the source of love, light, truth, as we know it here, we must go out beyond the limits of this shadowed world—to a Truth not mingled with its shadow, error —to a Life not mingled with its shadow, death—to a Love not mingled with its shadow, hate. We must seek for Pure Life, Pure Truth and Pure Love—and that is the definition of God.

◆§ ONE of the greatest mistakes is to think that contentment comes from something outside us rather than from a quality of the soul. There was once a boy who only wanted a marble; when he had a marble, he only wanted a ball; when he had a ball, he only wanted a top; when he had a top, he only wanted a kite, and when he had the marble, the ball, the top, and the kite, he still was not happy. Trying to make a discontented person happy is like trying to fill a sieve with water. However much you pour into it, it runs out too rapidly for you to catch up.

◆§ CONTENTMENT comes in part from faith— that is, from knowing the purpose of life and being assured that whatever the trials are, they come from the hand of a Loving Father. Secondly, in order to have contentment one must also have a good conscience. If the inner self is unhappy because of moral failures and unatoned guilt, then nothing external can give rest to the spirit. A third and final need is mortification of desires, the limitation of delights. What we over-love, we often over-grieve. Contentment enhances our enjoyment and diminishes our misery. All evils become lighter if we endure them patiently, but the greatest benefits can be poisoned by discontent. The miseries of life are sufficiently deep and extensive, without our adding to them unnecessarily.

◆§ JOY can be felt in both prosperity and adversity. In prosperity it consists not in the goods we enjoy but in those we hope for; not in the pleasures we experience but in the promise of those which we believe without our seeing. Riches may abound but those for which we hope are the kind which moths do not eat, rust consume, nor thieves break through and steal. Even in adversity there can be joy in the assurance that the Divine Master Himself died through the Cross as the condition of His Resurrection.

◄§ MEN live by their desires, but it is possible for us to choose whether we will desire things of the spirit or of the world. The man or woman who can look back on his day and count five times when he has refused to yield to some minute whim is on the way to inner growth: he has held himself back and rejected the slavery of things.

◄§ PHYSICAL IDLENESS deteriorates the mind; spiritual idleness deteriorates the heart. The joint action of air and water can turn a bar to rust. Therefore at every hour in the marketplace, man must ask himself: "Why stand I here idle?"

◄§ REVOLUTION within the soul is the Christian adventure. It requires no hatred, demands no personal rights, claims no exalted titles, tells no lies. In such a revolution, it is love which bores from within and acts as a Fifth Column, loyal to God, within our tangled and disordered selves. Such a revolution destroys the pride and selfishness, the envy and jealousy and longing to be "first" which makes us intolerant of others' rights. The sword it carries is not turned against our neighbor, but against our absurd over-valuation of the self. In other revolutions, it is easy to fight, for it is against the "evil enemy" that we are at war. But the Christian revolution is difficult, for the enemy we must assault is a part of us. Yet this is the only revolution that ever issues in true peace: other rebellions are never ended, for they stop short of their goal: they leave hatred still simmering in the soul of man.

◄§ EVERY LOVE rests on a tripod. Every love has three bases or supports: goodness, knowledge and similarity.

„§ EVERYONE must have pleasure, the philosophers tell us. The man who has integrated his personality in accordance with its nature, and oriented his life towards God knows the intense and indestructible pleasure the saints called joy. No outward event can threaten him or ruffle his happiness. But many men look outward for their pleasure and expect the accidents of their lives to provide their happiness. Since nobody can make the universe his slave, everyone who looks outward for pleasure is bound to disappointment. A glut of entertainment wearies us; a realized ambition becomes a bore; a love that promised full contentment loses its glamour and its thrill. Lasting happiness can never come from the world. Joy is not derived from the things we get or the people we meet; it is manufactured by the soul itself, as it goes about its self-forgetful business.

„§ MODERN MAN would be far happier if he would take a little time off to meditate. As the Old Testament prophet said: "Peace, peace and there is no peace, but no man considereth in his heart." The Gospel tells us that Our Blessed Lord withdrew Himself from the crowds into the wilderness and prayed. Martha, who was too busy about many things, was told that only one thing was necessary. A life of faith and with peace of soul can be cultivated only by periodical isolation from the cares of the world.

There are various kinds of weariness: weariness of the body, which can be satisfied under any tree or even on a pillow of stone; weariness of the brain, which needs the incubation of rest for new thought to be born; but hardest of all to satisfy is weariness of heart, which can be healed only by communion with God.

*nothing that is given in a spirit of
generosity is ever lost*

NOTHING that is given in a spirit of generosity is ever lost. In the materialist's reckoning, what is renounced is lost forever. In the realm of the spirit, this is not true. For what we give to God is not only recorded to us for eternal merit—it is even returned in this life. One of the most practical ways of assuring that we shall always have enough is to give and give and give in the Name of the Lord. Similarly, the most rapid increase in love of God can be obtained by being totally generous to our neighbors. *"Give and the gifts will be yours; good measure, pressed down and shaken up and running over, will be poured into your lap; the measure you award to others is the measure that will be awarded to you."* (LUKE 6:39.)

The use to which we put what we have is closely related to what we are, to our "being," and to what we will become. He who keeps everything he has for himself, must lose it all at death; he who has given it away will get it back in the coin of immortality and joy.

✳ G I V E away money to those who are in need, for by relieving their necessity you will make friends of those who will intercede for the salvation of your soul. Money will not buy heaven; but it will make friends for us that will help us when we fail. "Inasmuch as you do it to the least of these my brethren, you did it unto me." Those who have been helped by our charity will lead us before the throne saying: "This is he of whom we have spoken and who did so much for us in the life below."

✳ W E M E N and women are not wise enough nor innocent enough to judge each other. And the only decision we can rightly make about our brother who is doing wrong is to admit it and to say, "We will leave him to God."

✳ D I S S A T I S F A C T I O N sometimes can be the motive of true progress. Dissatisfied with the pen, man invented the printing press; dissatisfied with the chariot and the locomotive, he invented the airplane. There is implanted in everyone an impulse which drives the spirit to beat its wings like an imprisoned eagle in the cages of this earth until there is blood on its plumes. Did hearts but analyze this urge that is within them, which drives them away from the actual to the possible and makes them dig in the desert of their lives for new living springs, and climb every mountain to get a better look at heaven, they would see that they are being drawn back again to God, from Whom they came.

✳ P L E A S U R E S must be arranged in a hierarchy if we are to get the greatest enjoyment out of life. The most intense and lasting joys come only to those who are willing to practice a certain self-restraint, to undergo the boredom of a preliminary discipline. The best view is from the mountaintop, but it may be arduous to reach it. No man ever enjoyed reading Horace without drilling himself with the declensions of his grammar first. Full happiness is understood only by those who have denied themselves some legitimate pleasures in order to obtain deferred joys. Men who "let themselves go," go to seed or go mad. The Saviour of the world Himself told us that the best joys come only after we have purchased them by prayer and fasting: we must give up our copper pennies first, out of love for Him, and He will pay us back in pieces of gold, in joy and ecstasy.

✳ I f o n the last day we would receive a merciful judgment, we must begin here below to be merciful to others. Just as the clouds release only the moisture which they gathered from the earth, so too can Heaven release only the mercy we have sent heavenward.

✳ E v e r y t a s k we undertake has two aspects— our purpose, which makes us think it worth doing, and the work itself, regarded apart from its end-purpose. We play tennis to get exercise; but we play the game as well as possible, just for the joy of doing the thing well. The man who argued that he could get as much exercise by sloppy technique on the courts would have missed an understanding of the second aspect of all activity: the accomplishment of the task in accordance with its own standards of excellence. In the same way, a man working in an automobile factory may have, as his primary purpose, the earning of wages; but the purpose of the work itself is the excellent completion of the task. A workman should be aware of the second purpose at all times—as the artist is aware of the aim of beauty in his painting and the housewife is aware of the need for neatness when she dusts.

✳ T h e legitimate pride in doing work well relieves it of much of its drudgery. Some people, who have held to this craftsman's standard, get a thrill from any job they do. They know the satisfaction of "a job well done" whether they are engaged in caning a chair or cleaning a horse's stall or carving a statue for a Cathedral. Their honor and their self-respect are heightened by the discipline of careful work. They have retained the old attitude of the middle ages, when work was a sacred event, a ceremony, a source of spiritual merit. Labor was not then undertaken merely for the sake of economic gain, but was chosen through an inner compulsion, through a desire to project the creative power of God through our own human effort.

❋ WORK is a moral duty and not, as many men imagine, a mere physical necessity. St. Paul said, "*The man who refuses to work must be left to starve.*" When work is seen as a moral duty, it is apparent that it not only contributes to the social good, but also performs further services to the worker himself: it prevents the idleness from which many evils can arise and it also keeps his body in subjection to the reasoned will.

❋ WORK should, in justice, receive two kinds of reward—for it is not only individual, but also social. John Jones, who works in a mine, is tired at the end of the day: this is his individual sacrifice. For it he receives his wages. But John Jones has also, during the day, made a social contribution to the economic well-being of the country and the world. For this social contribution, John Jones today is given nothing . . . although he has a moral right to a share of the social wealth his work creates. We need a modification of the wage system, so that the worker may share in the profits, ownership or management of his industry. When labor leaders and capitalists thus agree together to give labor some capital to defend, there will no longer be two rival groups in industry; labor and management will become two cooperating members working together, as the two legs of a man cooperate to help him walk.

❋ WHEN God does answer your prayers of petition, do you ever thank Him for His gift?

❋ REPOSE—true leisure—cannot be enjoyed without some recognition of the spiritual world. For the first purpose of repose is the contemplation of the good . . . its goal is a true perspective one, the small incidents of everyday life in their relation to the larger goodness that surrounds us. Genesis tells us that after the creation of the world, *"God saw all that he had made, and found it very good."* Such contemplation of his work is natural to man, whenever he, too, is engaged in a creative task. The painter stands back from his canvas, to see whether the details of the seascape are properly placed. True repose is such a standing back to survey the activities that fill our days.

❋ HATRED comes from want of knowledge, as love comes from knowledge; thus, bigotry is properly related to ignorance.

❋ LIFE is not a snare nor an illusion. It would be that only if there were no Infinite to satisfy our yearnings. Everyone wants a Love that will never die and one that has no moments of hate or satiety. That Love lies beyond humans.

Human love is a spark from the great flame of Eternity. The happiness which comes from the unity of two in one flesh is a prelude to that great communion of two in one spirit. In this way, marriage becomes a tuning fork to the song of the angels, or a river that runs to the sea. Then it is evident that there is an answer to the elusive mystery of love and that somewhere there is a reconciliation of the quest and the goal, and that is in final union with God, where the chase and the capture, the romance and the marriage fuse into one. For since God is boundless, Eternal Love, it will take an ecstatic eternal chase to sound its depths.

❋ THERE are few things more beautiful in life than to see that deep passion of man for woman which begot children as the mutual incarnation of their love, transfigured into that deeper "passionless passion and wild tranquility" which is God.

* MOST PEOPLE in the world are unloved. Some do not make themselves lovable because of their selfishness; others do not have enough Christian spirit to love those who do not love them. The result is that the world is full of lonely hearts. Here we speak not of love in the romantic or carnal sense, but in the higher sense of generosity, forgiveness, kindness and sacrifice.

* THERE ARE some people who love to boast of their tolerance, but actually it is inspired by egotism; they want to be left alone in their own ideas, however wrong they be, so they plead for a tolerance of other people's ideas. But this kind of tolerance is very dangerous, for it becomes intolerance as soon as the ego is disturbed or menaced. That is why a civilization which is tolerant about false ideas instead of being charitable to persons is on the eve of a great wave of intolerance and persecution.

* TRADITIONALLY, all gossips are women; but men are often guilty of the same offense. They call it "judging."

* WE love to see ourselves idealized in the minds of others. That is one of the beautiful joys of love. We become fresh, innocent, brave, strong in the mind of the beloved. Love covers up the corruption of the soul. The winter of discontent is forgotten by being clothed in the blossoms of a new spring. After a while the lover begins to substitute what he really is in his own mind, with what he is in the mind of the other. It is this idealization which pleases in love. That is why love gives an incentive to betterment. When the other thinks well of us, we try to be worthy of that opinion. The fact that others assume us to be good is a great incentive to goodness. That is why too,

26

one of the basic principles of life ought to be to assume goodness in others; thus we make them good.

✷ K N O W L E D G E is in the mind; character is in the
will. To pour knowledge into the mind of a child, without
disciplining his will to goodness, is like putting a rifle into the
hands of a child. Without education of the mind a child could
be a stupid devil. With education of the mind, but without love
of goodness, a child could grow up to be a clever devil.

✷ E L D E R S must not be too critical of the teen-
agers, particularly when they rebel against them. From one
point of view they are not in rebellion against restraint, but
against their elders for not giving them a goal and purpose of
life. The teen-ager's protest is not conscious. He does not know
why he hates his parents, why he is rebellious against authority,
why his fellow teen-agers are becoming more and more delin-
quent. But the real reason is under the surface; it is an unconscious protest against a society which has not given him a pattern of life. The schools he attends have never stressed restraint,
discipline or self-control. Many of the teachers have defined
freedom and even democracy as the right to do whatever you
please. When this temporary phase of rebellion is past, the teen-
agers will look for some great cause to which they can make a
a total dedication. They must have an ideal. In many instances
today, they have no greater object of worship than to wrap
their emotional lives around a movie hero, a movie star, a band
leader or a crooner. This sign of decaying civilizations will pass
when the catastrophe comes. Then youth will look for a different type to imitate, namely, either heroes or saints.

✷ A N G E R is no sin under three conditions: (1) If
the cause of anger be just, for example, defense of God's honor;
(2) if it be no greater than the cause demands, that is, if it be
kept under control; and (3) if it be quickly subdued: "Let not
the sun go down upon your anger."

✳ MANY PEOPLE today have taken as their goal the obtainment of wealth. This is an inferior "destination," for it reduces man's dignity, making him serve something lesser than himself—for material goods are inferior to human personality. Other people chase after honors, publicity and fame. These are also unsatisfying and unworthy goals; anyone who steps into a shower, where he cannot carry his press-clippings, knows that his celebrity has not elevated him above other men. To make "what people say" an aim in life is to court a nervous breakdown by becoming the slave of every copywriter's whim.

✳ OUR LORD never tried to induce the poor to accept poverty as a good, or misery as a thing to be sought for itself. He glorified neither the poor man nor the rich man. But the one He did praise was the poor man who, having once been rich, had willingly made himself poor . . . the poor man who, by detaching himself from everything, became possessed of everything—the man who, wanting nothing, owned all things. For Our Lord does not canonize the "giving up" of wealth in favor of a vacuum; He approves, rather, of giving wealth in exchange for the far greater riches of Heaven. He did not tell us "Blessed are the poor," or "Blessed are the rich." But He told us, "Blessed are the poor in spirit."

✳ EVIL is always mutilation of the self. If I live as I ought to live, I become a man; if I live as my whims dictate, I become a beast, and an unhappy beast. This is not a result I ever planned, but it is still unavoidable. The man who wills to over-drink does not intend to ruin his health, but he does just that. The man who overeats does not count on indigestion, but he gets it. The man who wills to steal has not aimed at prison, yet that is where he lands.

When a traveler refuses to follow the guide-posts showing him the right way, he may still, eventually, reach his goal by finding disappointment at the end of every false trail. Disorder is a stern teacher, and a slow one, but a certain one. The Spanish have a proverb: *"He who spits against Heaven spits in his own face.*" Evil may triumph for a little while. It can win the first battle, but it loses the booty and the reward.

❋ THE atheist is properly defined as the person who has no invisible means of support.

❋ MODERN PSYCHOLOGY is based on the assumption that even in this world man really "gets away" with nothing. His secret hates, his hidden sins, his flippant treading upon the laws of morality—all of these leave their traces in his mind, his heart and his unconsciousness. Like the boy in the ancient fable who concealed in his blouse a fox which he had stolen. While denying his guilt, the fox ate away his entrails. The thousands of people stretched out on psychoanalytical couches may deny morality and guilt, but even while making their denial a real psychologist can see their mind being eaten away. There is nothing hidden that will not be revealed.

❋ PSYCHIATRY is not as much a modern discovery as it is a modern need. Its method has been known for centuries, but there was never the occasion to apply it, because in other ages men knew they could not "get away with it." Their purgations, reparations and amendments were settled on their knees in prayer, rather than on their back on a couch. But at that moment when the Divine and morality were denied, society came face to face with handling the mental effects which that very denial entailed. The crimes were not new, for people could snap their fingers just as much against the moral law in the days of faith as now. In those days when they did wrong, they knew it was wrong. They lost the road, but they never threw away the map. But today when men do wrong they call it right. This creates in addition to the moral problem which is denied, a *mental* problem. And that is where much psychiatry comes in. There is nothing new about the discovery that the reality we refuse to face we bury in our unconscious mind. What is new is the *need* to treat those who break the law and deny

the law; who live by freedom and refuse to accept its consequences.

✳ THE most current philosophy of life today is self-
expressionism: "Let yourself go"; "Do whatever you please."
Any suggestion of restraining errant impulses is called a masoch-
istic survival of the dark ages. The truth is that the only really
self-expressive people in the world are in the insane asylum.
They have absolutely no inhibitions, no conventions and no
codes. They are as self-expressive as hell, i.e., in complete disorder.

✳ THE alarming amount of hatred loose in the
modern world is largely caused by guilt: the man who hates himself soon begins to hate his fellowmen. Unconfessed, and sometimes unadmitted sins create a deep unease within the personality . . . the balance has to be, somehow, restored; the self
must somehow be placed in a more favorable light. The right
way to do this is to admit, confess and do penance for our sins.
The wrong way . . . which many unhappy people take today
. . . is to make the self seem better, sins and all, by detracting
from someone else. The individual who has injured someone he
loves often discovers that the act has turned his love to hate:
he can now appear innocent in his own eyes only if he accuses
the other of grave faults to justify the injury done him. To pass
thus from love to hatred is all too easy; but to turn hatred into
love is hard, for it can be done only if the self-deception is punc-
tured, the injury confessed.

✳ HATRED is hard to stop, for, if let alone, it sets
off a chain-reaction. One man's animosity arouses anger in
another, who, in turn, creates rage in someone else. That is why
Our Lord told us when we are struck on one cheek, to turn the
other: thus, by an interior effort of the will, we bring the chain
of anger to an end. The only way to destroy hate is for an individual to absorb it and, in his own heart, convert it into love.

✳ OUR RELATIONS with external things are all in terms of having or of not having; the inner life of the spirit centers, in contrast, on being, on what one is. Too often people spoil their whole lives in desires to *have,* when our main interests should be devoted to efforts to *be.* Since nothing in the material universe is greater than the spirit, the personality within each of us, every yielding of ourselves to some material craving or necessity is a loss. Having anything at all creates problems; the more keys a man carries on his key ring, the more numerous his problems. And not-having things we think we need can cause frustration, too. But the man who wants nothing is free; whatever happens to him is acceptable, and whatever is withheld from him is surrendered without a pang.

✳ THE men and women who, neglecting every effort to improve their souls, assert that they are happy anyway are merely lying to us and to themselves: their despair may be invisible, as yet, but it is latent and it is real. Let a crisis come upon such people, and the distress they concealed is evident enough. Suicides among those who lose their money or who are crossed in love reveal that only a thin, illusory substitute for the love of life saved them, until now, from their deep despair of the goodness of the universe.

✳ THERE are two barriers separating men from a happy destiny, and either one of them may cause a timid man or woman to hold back and sink into despair. Some men are unwilling to make the intellectual effort to seek truth for its own sake, to try to discover what this life is "all about," to humble their pride sufficiently to admit that God may be other than their present conception of Him, and that, to reach Him, they may still have many new things to learn and believe. That refusal holds back the proud from happiness. But there is another obstacle to belief: the refusal to admit Divinity because of the demands such a belief would make on us, and because we dare not face life without the habits of lust and avarice and selfishness which Faith would ask us to surrender.

31

✻ So long as mercy is available for all who despair of their own confusion and conflicts and inner incompleteness, it follows that sin is never the worst thing that can happen to a man. The worst thing is the refusal to recognize his sins. For if we are sinners, there is a Saviour. If there is a Saviour, there is a Cross. If there is a Cross, there is a way of appropriating it to our lives, and our lives to it. When that is done, despair is driven out and we have the *"peace which the world cannot give."*

✻ If we start with the belief that most people in the world are crooks, it is amazing how many crooks we find. If, however, we go into the world with the assumption that everyone is nice, we are constantly running into nice people. To a great extent the world is what we make it. We get back what we give. If we sow hate, we reap hate; if we scatter love and gentleness, we harvest love and happiness. Other people are like a mirror which reflects back on us the kind of image we cast. The kind man bears with the infirmities of others, never magnifies trifles and avoids a spirit of fault finding. He knows that the trouble with most people in the world is that they are unloved. No one cares for them either because they are ugly or nasty, or troublesome, or so-called bores. To a great extent their character is made by the resentment they feel to others who are unkind. One of life's greatest joys comes from loving those whom no one else loves. Thus do we imitate Our Heavenly Father Who certainly cannot see much in any of us creatures that is very attractive.

✻ Many psychiatrists today know very well that all they have to do to help certain distressed minds is to listen to their stories. Convince the anxious heart that you know the secret of his anxiety and he is already half cured. Even if we can convince the enemy that we have no bitterness in our heart against him, his arm will fall helpless at his side. All mental abnormalities have their roots in selfishness, all happiness has its roots in kindness. But to be really kind, one must see in everyone an immortal soul to be loved for God's sake. Then everyone is precious.

✻ MOST NEUROSES are bulwarks against fear. Many psychologists and physicians have come to adopt this thesis inasmuch as fear does provoke some kind of self-defense. It is actually not fear that is feared; the enemy is the tension between the conscience and what has happened. Fear is like the gauge on a steam boiler. It merely registers pressure.

✻ AVOIDING *the occasions of sin* is the easiest way of avoiding sin itself. The way to keep out of trouble is to keep out of the situations that lead up to trouble: the alcoholic must avoid the first sip of the first drink; the libertine must keep away from pretty women; the evil-minded must flee the company of those who degrade him. Our Lord said, "He that loveth the danger will perish therein." Temptation is hard to overcome at the last moment, when the sin is within our reach; it is easy to overcome if we act decisively to avoid a situation in which we might be tempted. Environments can make sin repulsive or attractive to us, for our surroundings affect us all. But we can *choose* the environment we wish and can ruthlessly reject the one that leads to trouble. Our Lord told us, "If thy right eye is the occasion of thy falling into sin, pluck it out and cast it away from thee." This means that if the books we read, the homes we visit, the games we play cause us to stumble morally, then we should cut them out and cast them from us.

✻ A DISAPPOINTMENT, a contradiction, a harsh word, an undeserved rebuke, a pain, a loss borne patiently in His name and endured as in His presence is worth more than any prayer said by the lips.

✻ THE divorce of mercy from justice is sentimentality, as the divorce of justice from mercy is severity. Mercy is not

33

love when it is divorced from justice. He who loves anything must resist that which would destroy the object of his love. The power to become righteously indignant is not an evidence of the want of mercy and love, but rather a proof of it. There are some crimes the tolerance of which is equivalent to consent to their wrong. Those who ask for the release of murderers, traitors, and the like, on the grounds that we must be "merciful, as Jesus was merciful," forget that that same Merciful Saviour also said that He came not to bring peace, but the sword. As a mother proves that she loves her child by hating the physical disease which would ravage the child's body, so Our Lord proves He loved Goodness by hating evil, which would ravage the souls of His creatures. For a doctor to be merciful to typhoid germs or polio in a patient, or for a judge to be tolerant of rape, would be in a lower category the same as for Our Lord to be indifferent to sin. A mind that is never stern or indignant is either without love, or else is dead to the distinction between right and wrong.

❋ THE *basic error of mankind has been to assume that only two are needed for love: you and me, or society and me, or humanity and me. Really it takes three: self, other selves, and God; you, and me, and God.*

❋ THE reason why we are not better than we are is that we do not *will* to be better: the sinner and the saint are set apart only by a series of tiny decisions within our hearts. Opposites are never so close as in the realm of the spirit: an abyss divides the poor from the rich, and one may cross it only with the help of external circumstances and good fortune. The dividing line between ignorance and learning is also deep and wide: both leisure to study and a gifted mind would be required to turn an ignoramus into a learned man. But the passage from sin to virtue, from mediocrity to sanctity requires no "luck," no help from outer circumstances. It can be achieved by an efficacious act of our own wills in cooperation with God's grace.

St. Thomas tells us that, "We are not saints because we *will* not to be saints." He does not say, mind you, that we do not *want* to be saints: many of us do. But mere *wanting* is the wish that something shall come to pass without our acting to bring it about. *Willing* means that we plan to pay the necessary cost in effort and in sacrifice.

✳ M A N is the highest creature on earth: he matters more than every theory, every government, every plan, for the world and all that it contains are not worth one immortal soul. Let institutions crumble, blueprints go up in smoke, and governments decay. These are mere trivia, compared to the vast question asked of all of us: "How is a man the better for it, if he gains the whole world at the cost of losing his own soul?"

there can be no world peace
unless there is soul peace

U NLESS souls are saved, nothing is saved; there can be no world peace unless there is soul peace. World wars are only projections of the conflicts waged inside the souls of modern men, for nothing happens in the external world that has not first happened within a soul.

‌ MATTER divides, as spirit unites. Divide an apple into four parts and it is always possible to quarrel as to who has the biggest part; but if four men learn a prayer, no one man deprives the other of possessing it—the prayer becomes the basis of their unity. When the goal of civilization consists, not in union with the Heavenly Father, but in the acquisition of material things, there is an increase in the potentialities of envy, greed, and war. Divided men then seek a dictator to bring them together, not in the unity of love, but in the false unity of the three P's—Power, Police, and Politics.

◄§ MODERN MAN has locked himself in the prison of his own mind; and only God can let him out, as He let Peter out of his dungeon. All that man himself must do is to contribute the desire to get out. God will not fail; it is only our human desire that is weak. There is no reason for discouragement. It was the bleating lamb in the thickets, more than the flock in the peaceful pastures, which attracted the Saviour's heart and helping hand. But the recovery of peace through His grace implies an understanding of anxiety, the grave complaint of imprisoned modern man.

◄§ DO NOT think of God as always looking around corners with an angel as a secretary to jot down all your sins. He is also looking at your good deeds, seeing every drink of cold water you give in His name, every visit to the sick you make in His name, every act of kindness you do for your fellowman in His name.

◄§ IN EVERY human being, there is a double law of gravitation, one pulling him to the earth, where he has his time of trial, and the other pulling him to God, where he has his happiness. The anxiety underlying all modern man's anxieties arises from his trying to be himself without God or from his trying to get beyond himself without God. The example of the mountain climber is not exact, for such a man has no helper on the upper peak to which he aspires. Man, however, has a helper —God on the upper peak of eternity reaches out His Omnipotent Hand to lift him up, even before man raises his voice in plea. It is evident that, even though we escaped all the anxieties of modern economic life, even though we avoided all the tensions which psychology finds in the unconsciousness and consciousness, we should still have that great basic fundamental anxiety born of our creatureliness. Anxiety stems fundamentally from irregulated desires, from the creature wanting something that is unnecessary for him or contrary to his nature or positively harmful to his soul. Anxiety increases in direct ratio and proportion as man departs from God. Every man in the world has an anxiety complex because he has the capacity to be either saint or sinner.

☙ THE *Love of God is Mercifull*

If we had never sinned, we never could have called Christ "Saviour." "But thou hast mercy upon all, because thou canst do all things, and overlookest the sins of men for the sake of repentance. For thou lovest all things that are, and hatest none of the things which thou hast made: for thou didst not appoint, or make any thing hating it." (WISDOM 11:24, 25.)

☙ PEACE OF SOUL comes to those who have the right kind of anxiety about attaining perfect happiness, which is God. A soul has anxiety because its final and eternal state is not yet decided; it is still and always at the crossroads of life. This fundamental anxiety cannot be cured by a surrender to passions and instincts; the basic cause of our anxiety is a restlessness within time which comes because we are made for eternity. If there were anywhere on earth a resting place other than God, we may be very sure that the human soul in its long history would have found it before this. As St. Augustine has said, "Our hearts were made for Thee. They are restless until they rest in Thee, O God."

☙ TO BE a Christian means to be lifted out of the old humanity of Adam to the new humanity of Christ. As one cannot lead a physical life unless one is born to it, so one cannot lead a spiritual life unless one is born to it. No man is forced to accept that Christ Life any more than Mary was. It is free and consultive. Since that Divine Life in our souls is a pure gift of God, since it is not caused by any human effort or merited in the strict sense by anything we do, it, too, may be said to have had a Virgin Birth. As St. John tells the story, "He was in the world, and the world was made by him, and the world knew him not. He came unto his own, and his own received him not. But as many as received him, he gave them power to

39

be made the sons of God, to them that believe in his name: Who are born, not of blood, nor of the will of the flesh, nor of the will of man, but of God." (JOHN 1:10–13.)

❧ FELLOWSHIP with man is impossible without fellowship with God. Men cannot be brothers unless they have God as their common father, and God is not a Father unless He has a Son, according to whose Image we are made and in whose Spirit we are quickened and united.

❧ WHEN a person is tempted to evil, he must not think there is anything abnormal about him. A man is tempted, not because he is intrinsically evil, but because he is fallen man. No individual has a monopoly on temptation; everybody is tempted. Saints do not find it easy to be saints, and devils are not happy being devils. Not everybody is tempted in the same way: some are tempted to pervert the good instinct of self-preservation into egotism and selfishness; others, to pervert the good instinct of self-perpetuation through sex into lust; others are tempted to pervert the good instinct of self-extension through private property into avarice. And if one is tempted in any one of these three ways or in the way of intemperance, anger, envy, jealousy, gluttony, it is not because he is diseased: it is because, since the fall, goodness does not "come naturally," but with difficulty, and is overcome thoroughly only thanks to the supernatural.

❧ A CATHOLIC believes that remarriage after divorce and artificial birth control are wrong, not simply because the Church has so decreed, but because these practices are opposed to the natural law and to the supernatural law of Christ.

❧ MAN is animated by an urge, an unquenchable desire to enlarge his vision and to know the ultimate meaning of things. If he were only an animal, he would never use symbols, for what are these but attempts to transcend the visible? No, he is a "metaphysical animal," a being ever longing for answers to the last question. The natural tendency of the intellect toward truth and of the will toward love would alone signify that there is in man a natural desire for God. There is not a single striving or pursuit or yearning of the human heart, even in the midst of the most sensual pleasures, that is not a dim grasping after the Infinite. As the stomach yearns for food and the eye for light and the ear for harmony, so the soul craves God.

§ A CATHOLIC does not believe that man can forgive sins, but he does believe that God can forgive sins *through man*. Christ communicated to His Church: "Whose sins you shall forgive, they are forgiven them; and whose *sins* you shall retain, they are retained." (JOHN 20:23.)

§ GOD is not hard to find, because He gives Himself to us as the Divine Gift. Natural life itself is a gift. The soul has to come into the body from without, directly as a gift from the hands of God. And the supernatural life, too, is given to us from without. The whole meaning of Christianity is contained in the simple phrase of the creed, "He descended from Heaven." To each single soul, Our Lord addresses the words He spoke to the Samaritan woman at the well: "If thou didst know the gift of God, and who he is that saith to thee, Give me to drink; thou perhaps wouldst have asked of him, and he would have given thee living water." (JOHN 4:10.) As St. Paul told the Romans, "The grace of God, life everlasting, in Christ Jesus our Lord." (ROMANS 6:23.) And later on, to the Ephesians, "By grace you are saved through faith, and that not of yourselves, for it is the gift of God." (EPHESIANS 2:8.)

§ GOD is the most obvious fact of human experience.

◆§ THE truth of the matter is, not that God is hard to find, but rather that man is afraid of being found. That is why we so very often hear in Sacred Scripture the words "Fear not." At the very beginning of Divine life in Bethlehem, the angels found it necessary to warn the shepherds, "Fear not." In the midst of Our Lord's public life He had to tell his frightened Apostles, "Fear not." And after His Resurrection He had to preface His words on peace with the same injunction, "Fear not."

Our Lord finds it necessary to warn us not to fear because there are three false fears that keep us away from God: (1) We want to be saved, but not from our sins. (2) We want to be saved, but not at too great a cost. (3) We want to be saved in *our* way, not His.

◆§ THERE has been no single influence which has done more to prevent man from finding God and rebuilding his character, has done more to lower the moral tone of society than the denial of personal guilt. This repudiation of man's personal responsibility for his action is falsely justified in two ways: by assuming that man is only an animal and by giving a sense of guilt the tag "morbid."

◆§ IF THE sense of guilt is an estrangement from God and sorrow at having wounded someone we love, if the ache of self-reproach is a symptom of our rejection of love's invitation, then our emphasis must be not so much on the guilt, as on the way to remove it and find peace. It takes love to see that love has been hurt. Divine Love always rewards that recognition by forgiveness; and once the forgiveness is given, a relationship is restored in a much more intimate way than ever before. There is more joy, Our Lord said, among the Angels of Heaven for one sinner doing penance than for the ninety-nine just who needed not penance.

◆§ TO THE extent that psychoanalysis, in the twentieth century, takes an interest in the inside of a man's soul, it represents a great progress over the sociologies of the nineteenth century, which thought that everything that was wrong in the world was due to poverty, bad economic conditions, free trade, high tariffs, or politics. Furthermore, to the extent that psychoanalysis has revealed the effects of our minds—even of the unconscious mind—on our physical health and behavior, it has confirmed the great Christian truth that an uncontrolled mind (or even an uncontrolled unconsciousness) leads to abnormality.

◄§ TRUE Christian greatness is measured not by superiority, but by service: "And he that will be first among you, shall be your servant." (MATTHEW 20:27.) The greatest race on earth is the race that renders the most service to others in the name of God.

◄§ THE examination of conscience brings to the surface the hidden faults of the day; it seeks to discover the weeds that are choking the growth of God's grace and destroying peace of soul. It is concerned with thoughts, words, and deeds, with sins of omission and sins of commission. By omission we mean the good that is left undone—a failure to aid a needy neighbor, a refusal to offer a word of consolation to those who are burdened with sorrow. Sins of commission involve malicious remarks, lies, acts of dishonesty, and those seven sins which are the seven pallbearers of the soul: self-love, inordinate love of money, illicit sex, hate, overindulgence, jealousy, and laziness. In addition to all this, there is the examination for what spiritual writers call our "predominant fault." Every person in the world has one sin which he commits more than others. Spiritual directors say that if we blotted out one great sin a year in a short time we should be perfect.

◄§ THERE has never been in the history of the Church a saint who was not joyful: there have been many saints who were great sinners, like Augustine, but there have never

43

been sad saints. This is understandable: perhaps there could not be anything in life more depressing than the knowledge that one has been guilty of a grave sin, without the chance Christians enjoy of starting all over again. St. Paul wisely distinguishes between the sadness of the guilty who know Redemption and the depression of those who deny both their guilt and the possibility of forgiveness. "For the sorrow that is according to God worketh penance, steadfast unto salvation; but the sorrow of the world worketh death." (II CORINTHIANS 7:10.) "For know ye that afterwards, when he desired to inherit the benediction, he was rejected; for he found no place of repentance although with tears he had sought it." (HEBREWS 12:17.)

§ THE correct definition of a good Catholic is a Catholic who takes the salvation of his soul seriously.

§ A FEW decades ago, nobody believed in the confession of sins except the Church. Today everyone believes in confession, with this difference: some believe in confessing their own sins; others believe in confessing other people's sins. The popularity of psychoanalysis has nearly convinced everyone of the necessity of some kind of confession for peace of mind. This is another instance of how the world, which threw Christian truths into the wastebasket in the nineteenth century, is pulling them out in isolated, secularized form in the twentieth century, meanwhile deluding itself into believing that it has made a great discovery. The world found it could not get along without some release for its inner unhappiness. Once it had rejected confession and denied both God and guilt, it had to find a substitute.

§ THE spirit of confession is not one of fact finding, but of mercy. If man himself accords pardon to others who humbly avow their faults, why should not God do the same? That is precisely what Our Blessed Lord has done. He has taken the natural avowal of faults—which already has an expiatory force

44

—and has elevated it to the dignity of a Sacrament. Avowal is only human, but He has divinized it. What is natural, He has made supernatural. The indispensable condition of receiving human pardon—the open avowal of guilt—is the condition upon which Almighty God grants His pardon in the Sacrament of Mercy. With infinite tenderness, He told the story of the prodigal son who came back to his father, acknowledged his guilt, and was rewarded with the embrace and kiss of his father. Such is the joy of God at a sinner's return, for "even so there shall be joy in heaven upon one sinner that doth penance, more than upon ninety-nine just who need not penance." (LUKE 15:7.)

    ⁝ T H E great advantage of the confessional is that the confession is kept absolutely secret. Every priest is bound by the *sigillum*, or seal, which forbids him, even under penalty of death, to reveal a person's confession in even the most general way. Knowing this is a great consolation for a penitent, who recognizes that his personality has a right to secrecy and who does not want to see his confidences revealed in a book of "case histories." Nothing so much wrecks one's confidence as the discovery that he has divulged his secrets to the wrong persons. Out of that betrayal and prostitution a new shame is born which makes future confidences impossible for him.

    ⁝ A s o u l that has confessed its guilt wants an ideal to strive toward—and an ideal more inspiring than "what everyone approves" in our society. This the confessional offers in the Supreme Example of the Person of Our Lord, Who gives us His grace to amend our lives through sorrow and repentance.

    ⁝ T H E R E is no surer formula for discontent than to try to satisfy our cravings for the ocean of Infinite Love from the teacup of finite satisfactions. Nothing material, physical, or carnal can ever satisfy man completely; he has an immortal soul which needs an Eternal Love. "Not by bread alone doth man live." Man's need for Divine Love, once perverted, impels him to go on seeking Infinite Love in finite beings—never finding it, yet not able to end the search despite his disappointments. Then follow cynicism, boredom, ennui, and finally despair. Having lost spiritual oxygen, such a man suffocates. Life ceases to mean anything precious to him, and he thinks of doing away with himself as his last and final act of rebellion against the Lord of Life.

&§ A REASON for the cult of sex is a desire to escape from the responsibility of living and from the unbearable voice of an uneasy conscience. By concentration upon the unconscious, animal, primitive areas, guilt-ridden individuals feel that they no longer need to fret about the meaning of life. Once God has been denied, then everything becomes permissible to them. By denying the ethical in life, they have substituted license for liberty.

&§ WHEN men believe in immortality, they not only seek the continuance of their spirit in eternity, but also the continuance of their flesh, through the creation of families which will survive them and meet the challenge death otherwise presents.

&§ THE equation of man with the animal is a great fallacy; sex in man is not the same as sex in animals. An animal feels, but no animal loves. In the animal, there is no body-mind conflict; in man, there is. In the animal, sex is mechanical, a matter of stimulus and response. In man, it is linked with mystery and freedom. In the animal, it is only a release of tension; in man, its occurrence is determined by no natural rhythm, but by the will. Sex can cause a loneliness and sadness in man which it cannot cause in an animal.

&§ SELF-PRESERVATION is one of the first laws of nature, and it implies a legitimate self-love; for if we did not

46

love ourselves, we could not continue to live. Our Divine Lord reminded us to love our neighbors *as we love ourselves*. Self-love, knowing it cannot exist by itself any more than the stomach can exist without food, extends itself in one direction by the acquiring of knowledge; and the more we know of the truth, the more our personality is developed. The quest for perfection of the self reaches to the infinite. No one has ever said, "I know enough." That is why we hate to have secrets kept from us (men hate this just as much as women). We are incurably curious; we were made to know.

&s AN UNDUE concentration upon a single one of life's activities tends to make a man abnormal through lopsidedness of interest. This is especially true of an excessive preoccupation with the carnal. It tends to make what is physical psychic, by tracing back everything to a single instinct. Sex in other ages was physical; it resulted in new life. Today, because it often thwarts life, it is also psychic. Sex is *thought about* as a medium of pleasure to such a degree that it has become an obsession.

&s FALSE isolation of the part from its whole is a common trait in contemporary thought. Man's life nowadays is divided into many compartments which remain ununited and unintegrated. A businessman's business has no connection with his life in the family—so little in fact that his wife (his "little wife") is kept ignorant of her husband's income. As there is no connection between a man's profession and the rest of his daily existence, neither is there a connection between his daily life and his religion. This chopping up of life into watertight compartments becomes more disastrous as occupation and work are related less and less to a strictly human ideal; mechanization plays a catastrophic role.

&s THE sex drive in man is *at no moment* an instinct alone. Desire from its beginning is informed with spirit, and

47

never is one experienced apart from the other. The psychic and the physical interplay. Just as the idealists, who deny the existence of matter, sin against the flesh, so the sensualists and carnalists sin against the spirit. But to betray either aspect is to invite revenge. "Our body is a part of the universal order created and preserved by God. Rightly viewed, it is itself a self-contained universe entrusted to us as a limited but sacred property. The most substantial sin is that which we commit against ourself and especially against our own body. The offense against our own body includes a sin against the Creator."

❧ I T I S the Christian position that the sex instinct is the *reflection* of love in the spiritual order. The sun comes first, then its reflection in the pool. The voice is not a sublimation of the echo, and neither is the belief in God a sublimation of a carnal instinct. All love and all perfection and all happiness are first in God, then in things. The closer creatures, such as angels and saints, come to God, the happier they are; the farther away they stay, the less they can reveal the works of Divinity.

❧ T H E R E is a double love in each of us—a love that is self-realizing and looks to our own good, and a love that is self-effacing and looks to the good of another. Both loves are included in the Divine Command, "Thou shalt love thy neighbor as thyself." (MATTHEW 22:39.) The one love is self-assertive and possessive—it makes us eat, drink, and work to sustain our life. The other love is sacrificial or possessed and seeks not to own but to be owned, not to have but to be had. The first takes water that it may live. The other shares or even gives up the water that the neighbor may live.

❧ H o w life changes its meaning when we see the love of the flesh as the reflection of the Eternal Light shot through the prism of time! They who would separate the earthly sound from the heavenly harp can have no music; they who believe that love is only the body's breath soon find love breathes its last and they have made a covenant with death. But they who see in all earthly beauty the faint copy of Divine loveliness, they who see in fidelity to every vow, even when the other is untrue, a proof that God loves us who are so unlovable, they who, in the face of their trials, see that God's love ended in a cross, they who allow the river of their rapture to broaden out the blended channels of prayer and worship—these will, even on earth, learn that Love was made flesh and dwelled amongst us. Thus, Love becomes an ascension toward that blessed day when the limitless depths of our souls will be filled with the boundless giving, in one eternal now, where love is life's eternity and God is Love.

◆§ A CATHOLIC believes that Our Lord is present in the Eucharist in every Catholic church. That is why he tips his hat when he passes a church. That is why he genuflects when he enters the church. That is why there are kneeling benches in church; for adoration is physically expressed by the humility of kneeling.

◆§ CHRISTIANITY says that the repression of evil thoughts, desires, and acts—such as the urge to kill, despoil, calumniate, rob, injure, covet, hate—is good for the soul; it deplores the repression of guilt or sin through a denial of the need of confession. And it states that the repression of actual graces, inspirations to a good life, and the urge to sacrifice self for neighbor is bad for the soul.

Christianity does not believe that the repression of the sex instinct is good. But it does believe in repressing the *abuse* of these instincts, so as to prevent lust in the one case and gluttony in the other. The Church has never taught that man is made up principally of two levels, the conscious and the unconscious; she states that there are three levels, body, soul, and the desire of God. Man is not just a beast, subject to the claims of his animal instincts; he has also ethical and spiritual selves which demand expression according to their natures. But this is not always easy.

◆§ HAPPINESS consists in overcoming the bias to evil by realizing one's Divine vocation and by overcoming the urge of nature; and this is not achieved through the orgiastic release of primeval forces, but rather through an *askesis* which amounts almost to violence. This is what Our Blessed Lord had in mind when He said that the Kingdom of Heaven suffereth violence and only the violent will bear it away. To the Christian, the way of perfection is the way of discipline, because he understands perfection as the satisfaction of personality in its highest reaches—namely, the attainment of life and truth and love, which is God.

◆§ THERE is nothing so dangerous for a civilization as softness, and there is nothing so destructive of personality as a want of discipline. Arnold Toynbee, the historian, tells us that, out of twenty-one civilizations which have vanished, sixteen collapsed because of decay within. Nations are not often murdered; they more often commit suicide. That is the sinister meaning of our present mood of selfishness and love of pleasure, our affirmation of our own egotism, our widespread refusal to discipline the self. Although two world wars have imposed upon us many sacrifices which we have accepted willingly, even these have not been sufficient to make us perform the greatest sacrifice of all—to give up the illusion that a man is most self-expressive when he allows the animal to gain mastery over the spirit.

◆§ THE accidents of life, such as political position, wealth, education, are not occasions for pride, but opportunities for service: "To reveal his Son in me, that I might preach him among the Gentiles, immediately I condescended not to flesh and blood." (GALATIANS 1:16.)

&§ P E A C E is a fruit of love, and love flowers in the man oriented toward God. The greatest privilege that can come to man is to have his life God-directed; this follows when he has remotely paved the way by disciplined self-direction. God cares enough for us to regulate our lives—and this is the strongest proof of love that He could give to us. For it is a fact of human experience that we do not care very much about the details of other people's lives unless we love them. We are not deeply interested in hearing more of those individuals whom we meet in the subway and in the street and on the highway. But as soon as we begin to know and love any of them, then we become more and more interested in their lives; we have a greater care for them. As we bring them into the area of our love, both our interest and their happiness increases. It is like this when we bring ourselves into the area of God's love: there is an increasing Divine guidance of the details of our life, and we are ever being made more sure of the depth and reality of His Love.

&§ C H R I S T I A N self-discipline is really self-expression—expression of all that is highest and best in self; the farmer plows under the weeds for the completest expression of the corn's desire to grow. Self-control, through mortification or asceticism, is not the rejection of our instincts, passions, and emotions, nor is it thrusting these God-given impulses into unconsciousness, as the materialists accuse the Christians of doing. Our passions, instincts, and emotions are *good*, not evil; self-control means only curbing their inordinate excesses.

&§ O N E of the cruellest things that can happen to a human being is to be tolerated. Never once did Our Lord say, "Tolerate your enemies!" But He did say, "Love your enemies; do good to them that hate you." (MATTHEW 5:44.) Such love can be achieved only if we deliberately curb our fallen nature's animosities.

&§ T H E secret of peace of soul is to combine detachment from evil with attachment to God, to abandon egotism as the ruling, determining element in living and to substitute Our Divine Lord as the regent of our actions. What is anti-God must be repressed; what is Godly must be expressed. Then one will no longer awaken with a dark brown taste in the mouth or a feeling of being rundown at the heels. Instead of greeting each day with the complaint, "Good God, morning!" he will say, from the happiness of a soul in love, "Good morning, God!"

᪗ WHEN there are seven people in a room, few ever refer to the fact that there are fourteen arms present. But if we found a detached arm lying in a corner, it would create consternation; it is a problem only because it is detached. A soul isolated from God is like that arm. Its conscience (to take another example) is like a broken anklebone; it hurts because it is not where it ought to be. The final stage of this sadness resulting from man's unrelatedness to God is a desire to die, combined with a fear of death—for "conscience doth make cowards of us all."

᪗ FOR the sinner to be made well confession and sorrow are required. And the sorrow must have in it an appeal to God's mercy to distinguish it from remorse. St. Paul makes the distinction in writing to the Corinthians: "For the sorrow that is according to God worketh penance, steadfast unto salvation; but the sorrow of the world worketh death." (II CO-RINTHIANS 7:10.) Remorse, or "the sorrow of the world," results in worry, jealousy, envy, indignation; but sorrow related to God results in expiation and hope. Perfect sorrow comes from a sense of having offended God, Who is deserving of all our love; this sorrow or contrition, felt in confession, is never a vexing, fretful sadness which depresses, but it is a sadness from which great consolation springs. As St. Augustine put it, "The penitent should ever grieve, and rejoice at his grief."

᪗ THE capacity for conversion is greater in the really wicked than in the self-satisfied and complacent. The very emptiness of soul of the sinners is in itself an occasion for receiving the compassion of God. Self-disgust is the beginning of conversion, for it marks the death of pride.

◄§ F E W consolations are greater than the knowledge that we are bound up in a great corporation of prayers and sacrifices. The Communion of Saints is the great discovery of those who, as adults, find the fullness of faith. They discover that for years there have been dozens, in some instances hundreds, of souls praying especially for them—storming heaven with the plea that a little act of humility by the convert might open a crack in his armor to let in God's grace and truth. Every soul in the world has a price tag on it, and since many cannot or will not pay the price themselves, others must do it for them. There is probably no other way to account for the conversion of some souls than the fact that in this world, as in the next, their parents, relatives, or friends interceded to God and won for them the prize of everlasting life.

◄§ T H E Christian principle for conquering death is twofold: (1) Think about death. (2) Rehearse for it by mortification now. The purpose of contemplation is to conquer the dread and compulsion of death by voluntarily facing it. Through anticipating the final end, we may contemplate new beginnings. Our Blessed Lord lived from the end of life backward: "I came to give My life for the redemption of the world." The Lamb is pictured as "slain from the beginning of the world."

◄§ D E A T H can be robbed of its greatest fearfulness if we practice for it. Christianity recommends mortification, penance, and detachment as a rehearsal for the great event. For every death should be a great masterpiece, and, like all masterpieces, it cannot be completed in a day. A sculptor who wishes to carve a figure out of a block uses his chisel, first cutting away great chunks of marble, then smaller pieces, until he finally reaches a point where only a brush of hand is needed to reveal the figure. In the same way, the soul has to undergo tremendous mortifications at first, and then more refined detachments, until finally its Divine image is revealed. Because mortification is recognized as a practice of death, there is fittingly inscribed on the tomb of Duns Scotus, *Bis Mortuus; Semel Sepultus* (twice died, but buried only once). When we die to something, something comes alive within us. If we die to self, charity comes alive; if we die to pride, service comes alive; if we die to lust, reverence for personality comes alive; if we die to anger, love comes alive.

◄§ CATHOLICS build their own schools, while paying taxes for non-religious schools, because they want their children to be educated in the love of Christ and His moral law, and thus to save their souls and become worthy citizens of their country.

◄§ DEATH is meant to be our true birth, our beginning. Christianity, in contrast to paganism, always blesses her children's spiritual birth into eternity; in the liturgy, the day on which a saint dies is called his *natilitia*, or birthday. The world celebrates a birthday on the day a person is born to physical life; the Church celebrates it when a person is born to eternal life. There are only three exceptions to this, and they were made for very good reasons: the only physical birthdays in the liturgy are those of Our Divine Lord (December 25), of the Blessed Mother (September 8), and of St. John the Baptist (June 24). This is because each of these births marked a special infusion of Divine Life into the world: our Lord *is* Eternal Life; the Blessed Mother, through Her Immaculate Conception, participated in that Eternal Life from the first moment of Her Conception; and St. John the Baptist was sanctified in his mother's womb when he was visited by His Lord, still tabernacled within the Blessed Mother. These three exceptions rather prove than contradict the rule that life comes through death, spirituality through mortification, and the saving of the soul in eternity through the losing of it in time.

◆§ E v e r y conversion starts with a crisis: with a moment or a situation involving some kind of suffering, physical, moral, or spiritual; with a dialectic, a tension, a pull, a duality, or a conflict. This crisis is accompanied, on the one hand, by a profound sense of one's own helplessness and, on the other hand, by an equally certain conviction that God alone can supply what the individual lacks.

◆§ G o d becomes a possibility to the despairing soul only as it begins to see that it can do "all things in Him Who strengtheneth me." The naturally good man of Rousseau and Liberalism, the harmless egotist of Adam Smith, and the prudently selfish man of John Stuart Mill do not feel these moral tensions, particularly when their lives are cushioned in comfort. It has taken a century for followers of these false optimists to sense that their inner vacancy results from a freedom yearning for the infinite, yoked to a finiteness whose essence is disgust. A new self is needed, and man cannot renovate himself. No vague humanism, no busy dedication to social causes, can root out the sense of guilt—because guilt implies a *personal* relationship with God. And a personal relationship implies love. For us to become truly moral, there must be a surrender to an all-loving Christ Who can do what no man can do. And then the pain passes away: though the emptiness of soul that sin has given us sees itself confronted by Christ, the emphasis is immediately shifted from our sin to His mercy, from self to the Cross.

◆§ C o n v e r s i o n from mediocrity to a full surrender is no easier than the conversion from sin to charity; in either case, there is the plucking out of an eye and the cutting off of an arm. It seems to the convert that he is asked to give up everything—not only all he has, but even control over his mind—but this is because he does not yet understand the joyous freedom of union with God. Pleasures of the flesh are always greater in anticipation than in realization, but the joys of the spirit are always greater in realization than in anticipation.

≈§ T o d a y there is in the world a vast army of good souls who have not yet entered into the fullness of the crisis; they are thirsty, but they fear to ask Him for a drink lest He pour it from a chalice. They are cold, but they fear drawing near His fires, lest those flames cleanse as they illumine them; they know that they are locked in the sepulchers of their own pettiness, but they fear that their Resurrection, like His, will bear the scars of battle. There are many who would like to stretch a finger to Our Lord; they shrink back lest He should seize their hands and woo their hearts. But they are not far from the Kingdom of God. Already, they have the desire; they need only the courage with which to pass through the crisis in which, through an apparent surrender, they will find themselves victors in the captivity of Divinity.

≈§ G o d never refuses grace to those who honestly ask for it. All He asks is that the vague thirst for the Infinite which has urged the soul on to seek its good in a succession of pleasures shall now be transformed into a thirst for God Himself. All we need do is to voice these two petitions: Dear Lord, illumine my intellect to see the Truth, and give me the strength to follow it. It is a prayer that is *always* answered. And it makes no difference whether the desire for God we voice has come from our disgusts, satieties, and despair or whether it is born of our love of the beautiful, the perfect. God is willing to take either our old bones or our young dreams, for He loves us, not because of the way we are, but because of what we can be through His grace.

A S all men are touched by God's flaming love, so all are also touched by the desire for His intimacy. No one escapes this longing; we are all kings in exile, miserable without the Infinite. Those who reject the grace of God have a desire to *avoid* God, as those who accept it have a desire *for* God.

✻ H o w does man begin to live the higher life in God? First of all, God must come down to him, the Eternal must invade human history: this is the meaning of the Incarnation. Second, man must himself surrender his lower nature. But here there appears a difference between man and all other creatures —man is a *person*, which sunshine, grass, and cows are not. *Their* lower natures are destroyed by surrendering themselves to man, but since man is a person, his personality is indestructible. What man surrenders, then, is not his whole nature, but only that portion of it which is sinful, which is ungodlike. In conversion a man suffers a mortification, a kind of spiritual death, but his personality survives.

✳ THOSE who lack grace—that gift of God which is given so freely—have physical life but do not have spiritual life. This raises the question, "Why does not everyone accept grace?" The answer is to be found in the fact that man, alone in all nature, is free. The grass does not need to consult the moisture before it absorbs it to itself; the cow need not plead with the grass to come with it into the animal kingdom; but man is free, and God will break down no doors to force a higher destiny upon our wills. The Divine may only entreat and plead; He will show how much He loves us by dying to redeem us. But He will not use force, even to save us from our own shortsighted preference for a meaner share of life.

✳ A PERCEPTIBLE result of conversion is a *definite change in behavior and conduct of life*. Not only does conversion change one's values; it also reverses the tendencies and energies of life, directing them to another end. If the convert before conversion was already leading a good moral life, there is now less emphasis on keeping a law and more emphasis on maintaining a relationship of love. If the convert has been a sinner, his spiritual life frees him from habits and excesses which before weighed down the soul. He no longer need resort to alcohol or sleeping tablets. He often finds that these practices were not so much appetites as attempts to flee responsibility or to ensure, by plunging into unconsciousness, that he could avoid the necessity of choice. Before conversion, it was behavior which to a large extent determined belief; after conversion, it is belief which determines behavior. There is no longer a tendency to find scapegoats to blame for the faults of self, but rather a consciousness that the reformation of the world must begin with the reformation of self. There is still a fear of God, but it is not the servile fear a subject has for a dictator, but a filial fear, such as a living son has for a good father whom he would never wish to hurt. From such a Love one does not ever need to run away, and the previous acts of dissipation, which were disguised forms of flight, are now renounced.

❊ PHILOSOPHY gives a proof for the existence of God; the science of apologetics gives the motives for believing in Christ, the Son of God; but all the incontrovertible proofs they offer fall short of the certitude that actually comes to a convert through the gift of Faith.

❊ THOSE who have never gone through the experience of a complete conversion imagine that reason must be completely abdicated for such a step. We hear them make such remarks as, "I cannot understand it; he seemed like an intelligent man." But those who have gone through the experience of conversion see that just as the eye winks, closing itself to the light for an instant that it may reopen and see better, so, too, one winks his reason for that brief instant in which he admits that it may not know *all* the answers. Then, when faith comes, the reason is found to be intact and clearer sighted than before. Both reason and faith are now seen as deriving from God Himself; they can never, therefore, be in opposition. Knowing this, the convert loses all his doubts. His certitude in his faith becomes unshakable—indeed, it is his old notions which are now apt to be shaken by the earthquake of his faith.

❊ THE tragedy of the modern world is that so many deny sin. Never before in the history of the world was there so much evil, and never before was there so little consciousness of it. Talk to a modern man about reconciling his soul with God and he will say: "What have I ever done to Him? I let Him alone, why should He not leave me alone?"

❊ THE modern man is so confused that, for all his talk about freedom, he is often eager to renounce this gift in favor of security. Even when no greater security is offered him

59

in exchange, he is eager to give up his freedom of choice; he cannot bear the burden of its responsibility. Weary of being alone and afraid and isolated in a hostile world, he wants to surrender himself to something or to somebody—to commit a kind of mayhem of the will. Will he surrender to the anonymous authority of a collective state, or will he accept a spiritual authority which restores his freedom with the acceptance of truth?

The Church makes no man less free than he was before. But we chiefly value freedom in order to give it away; every man who loves surrenders his freedom, whether his passion be the love of a woman, the love of a cause, or the love of God.

✳ THERE is one simple way of beginning a conversion: cease asking what God will give you if you come to Him, and begin to ask what you will give God. It is not the sacrifice it sounds, for, in having Him, you will have everything besides.

✳ GOD could never let you suffer a pain, or a reversal, or experience sadness, if it could not in some way minister to your perfection. If He did not spare His own Son on the Cross for the redemption of the world, then you may be sure that He will sometimes not spare your wants, that you might be all you *need* to be: happy and perfect children of a loving Father. He may even permit us to wage wars as a result of our selfishness, that we may learn there is no peace except in Goodness and Truth.

✳ BECAUSE man turned his will against God, so now his passions and desires are turned against God's will. It is this fallen nature which all men have inherited. That is why the sin is called "original"—it came at the origin of human nature, and represents a loss, the soul registering a much greater loss than the body; for Man still has natural life, but he has not supernatural life.

It is right here that Christianity begins. In all other religions you have to be good to come to God. In Christianity you do not. Christianity is realistic: it begins with the fact that, whatever you are, you are not what you *ought* to be. If everything in the world were perfectly good, we would still need God, for all goodness comes from God. But the presence of evil makes that need more imperative. Christianity begins with the recognition that there is something in your life and in the world that *ought* not to be, that need not be, and that could be otherwise were it not for evil choices.

❊ RELIGION is not an individual affair! A man can no more have an individual religion than he can have an individual government or an individual astronomy or mathematics. Religion is social, and so social is it that it is not limited to the criminal class, as the thief believed, not to any class, race, nation, or color.

❊ WHAT does it mean to be a Christian? Christianity is not a system of ethics; it is a life. It is not good advice; it is Divine adoption. Being a Christian does not consist in being kind to the poor, going to Church, reading the Bible, singing hymns, being generous to relief agencies, just to employees, gentle to cripples, serving on Church committees, though it includes all of these. It is first and foremost a *love relationship*.

As you can never become a member of a family by doing generous deeds, but only by being born into it out of love, so you can never become a Christian by doing good things, but only by being born to it through Divine Love.

❊ WHEN you fail to measure up to your Christian privilege, be not discouraged for discouragement is a form of pride. The reason you are sad is because you looked to yourself and not to God; to your failing, not to His Love. You will shake off your faults more readily when you love God than when you criticize yourselves. The sick person looks happily at the physician, not at his wounds. You have always the right to love Him in your heart, even though now and then you do not love Him in your acts. Keep no accounts with God or you will always be so hopelessly in debt as to be bankrupt.

✳ St. paul tells us, not in a harsh, stoic manner, that if we are to live to Christ, we must "die daily." A happy death is a masterpiece and no masterpiece was ever perfected in a day. Dubois spent seven years in making the wax model for his celebrated statue of Joan of Arc. One day the model was finished and the bronze was poured into it. The statue stands today as a ravishing perfection of the sculptor's art. In like manner, our death at the end of our natural existence must appear as a ravishing perfection of the many years of labor we have given over to its mould by dying daily.

The greatest reason why we fear death is because we have never prepared for it. Most of us die only once when we should have died a thousand times—aye, when we should have died daily. Death is a terrible thing for him who dies only when he dies; but it is a beautiful thing for him who dies before he dies.

✳ Hate and love spring from the same passion, as laughter and sorrow drink from the same fountain of tears. The difference is in the motive and the end for which they live. Religion is something that must be either hated or loved. It cannot be watched!

✳ Judgment will be twofold. You will be judged at the moment of your death, which is the Particular Judgment, and you will be judged on the last day of the world, which is the General Judgment. The first Judgment is because you are a person and are, therefore, individually responsible for your free acts; your work will follow you. The second Judgment will be because you worked out your salvation in the context of a social order, and the mystical Body of Christ; therefore you must be judged by your repercussions upon it.

What will the Judgment be like, and here we refer to the Particular Judgment? It will be an evaluation of yourself as you really are. In each of us there are several persons: there is the person others think you are; there is the person *you* think you are; there is the person you *really are*.

✳ N o w what are you *really?* You are what you are, not by your emotions, your feelings, your likes and dislikes, but by your *choices*. The decisions of your free-will will be the content of your judgment.

We are all on the roadway of life in this world, but we travel in different vehicles: some in trucks, some in jeeps, some in ambulances; others in twelve cylinder cars, others in flivvers. But each of us does the driving.

✳ W H A T is Purgatory but a place or condition of temporal punishment for those who depart this life in God's grace, but are not entirely free from venial faults or have not entirely paid the satisfaction due to their transgressions? Purgatory is that place in which the Love of God tempers the Justice of God, and secondly, where the love of man tempers the injustice of man.

First, Purgatory is where the Love of God tempers the Justice of God. The necessity of Purgatory is grounded upon the absolute purity of God. In the Book of the Apocalypse we read of the great beauty of His City, of the pure gold, with its walls of jasper and its spotless light which is not of the sun nor moon but the light of the Lamb slain from the beginning of the world. We also learn of the condition of entering into the gates of that Heavenly Jerusalem: "There shall not enter into it anything defiled, or that worketh abomination, or maketh a lie, but they that are written in the book of the life of the Lamb."

✳ W H Y do moderns deny hell? Because they deny sin. If you deny human guilt, then you must deny the right of a state to judge a criminal, and the further right to sentence him to prison. Once you deny the sovereignty of law, you must necessarily deny punishment. Once you deny the sovereignty of God, you must deny hell.

The basic reason why moderns disbelieve in hell is because they really disbelieve in freedom and responsibility. To believe in hell is to assert that the consequences of good and bad acts are not indifferent. It does make a tremendous amount of difference to your body if you drink tea or TNT, and it makes a greater difference if your soul drinks virtue or vice.

⁂ HELL must be eternal. What is one thing life can never forgive? Death, because death is the negation of life. What is the one thing that Truth can never forgive? Error, for error is its contradiction. What is the one thing that Love can never forgive? It is the refusal to love, for hate would be the destruction and annihilation of love. That is why Hell is Eternal —it is the negation of Love.

⁂ THE clarity of vision and certitude of those who have the gift of faith is sometimes misunderstood even by those who have faith. Hence, a Catholic is sometimes impatient with one who has not the faith, wrongly thinking that the reason he sees the truth so clearly is because of his own innate cleverness, and the reason his neighbor does not see it is due either to his stupidity or his stubbornness. Faith, it must be remembered, is not due to our wisdom, and the lack of faith is not due to their ignorance. Faith is solely a gift of God. "Flesh and blood hath not revealed it to thee, but my Father who is in heaven." (MATTHEW 16:17.)

⁂ YOU have exactly the same eyes at night as you have in the day, but you cannot see at night, because you lack the additional light of the sun. So, too, let two minds with identically the same education, the same mental capacities, and the same judgment, look on a Host enthroned on an altar. The one sees bread, the other sees Christ, not, of course, with the eyes of the flesh, but with the eyes of faith. Let them both look on death: one sees the end of a biological entity, the other an immortal creature being judged by God on how it used its freedom. The reason for the difference is: one has a light which the other lacks, namely, the light of faith.

✻ PRIDE is of two kinds: it is either the pride of omniscience or the pride of nescience. The pride of omniscience tries to convince your neighbor you know everything; the new pride of nescience tries to convince your neighbor that he knows nothing. The latter is the technique used by "sophomores" who pride themselves on the fact that man can know nothing. Hence, they doubt everything, and of this they are very sure. They seem to forget that the doubting of everything is impossible, for doubt is a shadow, and there can be no shadow without light.

✻ THINK not that you lose your freedom by accepting the faith. A few years ago, I received a letter from a radio listener who said: "I imagine that you from your earliest youth were surrounded by priests and nuns who never permitted you to think for yourself. Why not throw off the yoke of Rome and begin to be free?"

I answered him thus: "In the center of a sea was an island on which children played and danced and sang. Around that island were great high walls which had stood for centuries. One day, some strange men came to the island in individual rowboats, and said to the children: Who put up these walls? Can you not see that they are destroying your freedom? Tear them down!

"The children tore them down! Now if you go there, you will find all the children huddled together in the center of the island, afraid to play, afraid to sing, afraid to dance—afraid of falling into the sea."

✻ EVERY moment comes to you pregnant with a Divine Purpose; time being so precious that God deals it out only second by second. Once it leaves your hands and your power to do with it as you please, it plunges into eternity, to remain forever whatever you made it.

❋ CIRCUMSTANCES must not control you; you must control circumstances. Do something to them! Even the irritations of life can be made stepping stones to salvation. An oyster develops a pearl because a grain of sand irritated it. Cease talking about your pains and aches. Thank God for them! An act of thanksgiving when things go against our will, then a a thousand acts of thanksgiving when things go according to our will.

Y O U will never be happy if your happiness
depends on getting solely what you want. Change the focus.
Get a new center. Will what God wills, and your joy no man
shall take from you. "So also you now indeed have sorrow; but I
will see you again, and your heart shall rejoice; and your joy
no man shall take from you. And in that day you shall not ask
me anything. Amen, amen I say to you: if you ask the Father
any thing in my name, he will give it you. Hitherto you have
not asked any thing in my name. Ask, and you shall receive;
that your joy may be full." (JOHN 16:22–24.)

◄§ T H E will, which is the seat of inclination, in belief, is never blind according to traditional philosophy. The intellect supplies its object and the reason of its belief, for nothing
is willed unless it is known. It will be recalled that, for St.
Thomas, the will is nobler than the intellect in those cases

where the object of the will is nobler than the soul. The reason is, that the intellect drags things down to its level, but the will always goes up to meet the requirements of its love. Thus it is nobler to love God than to know all created things, for in loving God the will goes out to meet God but in knowing things it descends to the finite and the material.

ঙ্চ THE *mind can know things beyond experience.*

ঙ্চ IT IS quite a remarkable fact that modern philosophers of science are in agreement with St. Thomas on the question of the value of empirical sciences. St. Thomas holds that inasmuch as they are based on incomplete induction, they can give only probable certitude. Our contemporaries hold that scientific conclusions are only provisory approximations of reality, and not its adequate representation. Such scientists as P. Duhem, H. Poincaré, G. Milhaud, E. Boutroux, E. Meyerson, Hugo Dingler, O. W. Richardson and others may differ in the detailed treatment they give to the problem, but at bottom all are in perfect agreement. Science does not penetrate into the essence or nature of physical things; this it leaves to the metaphysician. It is content to summarize in the most complete and commodious fashion data revealed by experience, describing rather than explaining.

ঙ্চ THE bigger a philosopher thinks he is, the less he thinks God is. The psychology of sainthood brings out this truth. The closer souls mount to God the less assured they are of their own importance, and the more certain they are of their own imperfection and nothingness. The reason for this is that as we get near the perfect and the infinite, the more clearly the defects of imperfect and the finite show forth, just as the closer we bring an object to the light the more its imperfections and defects are revealed. The contrary is equally true: the more a man exalts himself, the less God seems to him in comparison. The good man is never sure he is good because he measures himself by the Perfect; the evil man is quite sure he is good because he measures himself by himself.

⋅§ J u s t as water, ice and steam are all manifestations of the same substance; just as the length, breadth, and thickness of a cathedral do not make three cathedrals, but one; just as carbon, diamond and graphite are manifestations of one and the same nature; just as the color, perfume and form of a rose do not make three roses, but one; just as the soul, the intellect and the will do not make three lives, but one; just as $1 \times 1 \times 1 = 1$ and not 3, so in a much more mysterious way there are three Persons in the Blessed Trinity and yet only one God.

This is but the feeblest exposition of the mystery of the Trinity, but it may serve as a suggestion of the continuity of philosophy and theology.

⋅§ T h e mind must know, but it never knows anything fully until it knows God, and the least knowledge of God is worth more than the knowledge of all created things. If we knew what the sun was we would not need to know what its ray is; if we knew the ocean we would know the chemistry of a drop of water; if we knew the circle, we would know what the smallest arc is; and in knowing God we know all things.

⋅§ T h e Good Friday of twenty centuries ago did not mark the end of Him, as it did not mark the beginning. It is one of the moments of the Eternal Word of God. Jesus Christ has a prehistory—the only prehistory that is prehistory, a prehistory not to be studied in the rocks of the earth, not in the caves of man, not in the slime and dust of primeval jungles, but in the bosom of an Eternal Father; He alone brought history to history; He alone has dated all the records of human events ever since into two periods: the period before and the period after His coming; so that if we would ever deny that the Word became Flesh, and that the Son of God became the Son of man, we would have to date our denial as over one thousand nine hundred years after His coming.

◆§ AMERICA'S greatest enemy is not from without, but from within, and that enemy is hate: hatred of races, peoples, classes and religions. If America ever dies, it will be not through conquest but suicide.

It is heartening to know that there are many attempts to heal these wounds of hate. Principal among them are: pleas for tolerance, for the substitution of new hates, for example, Nazism, for the violent denunciation of groups as bigots. None of these remedies will eradicate hate. Tolerance pleas will not, for why should any creature on God's earth be tolerated? Substitution of other hatreds will not work, for you cannot cure small hates by big hates.

◆§ BY charity we do not mean kindness, philanthropy, generosity, or big-heartedness, but a supernatural gift of God by which we are enabled to love Him above all things for His own sake alone, and, in that love, to love all that He loves. To make it clear, we here set down the three principal characteristics of charity or supernatural love: (1) It is in the will, not in the emotions. (2) It is a habit, not a spasmodic art. (3) It is a love-relationship, not a contract.

◆§ BECAUSE charity is in the will, you can command it, which you cannot do with natural likes or dislikes. A little boy cannot help disliking spinach, as perhaps you cannot help disliking sauerkraut, and as I cannot help disliking chicken. The same is true of your reactions to certain people. You cannot help feeling an emotional reaction against the egotistical, the sophisticated, and the loud, or those who run for first seats or snore in their sleep.

Though you cannot *like* everyone because you have no control over your physiological reactions, you can *love* everyone in the Divine sense, for that kind of love, being in the will, can be commanded or elicited. That is why love of God and neighbor can be commanded: "A new commandment I give unto you: That you love one another, as I have loved you, that you also love one another." (JOHN 13:34.)

⋞ OVER and above your dislikes and your emotional reactions to certain people, there can coexist a genuine love of them, for God's sake. Charity is a consequence not of anything which affects our senses, but of Divine faith. Outwardly, your neighbor may be very unlikable; but inwardly he is one in whom the image of God can be recreated by the kiss of charity.

⋞ THERE is no Messianic race, no Messianic class, no Messianic color. Our Lord died for all men, and thus set up a new series of relationships with God. And from out of this new set of relationships, slum clearance and social justice and all the rest follow—but not otherwise.

⋞ HEAVEN is not a place where there is the mere vocal repetition of alleluias or the monotonous fingering of harps. Heaven is a place where we find the fullness of all the fine things we enjoy on this earth. Heaven is a place where we find in its plenitude those things which slake the thirst of hearts, satisfy the hunger of starving minds, and give rest to unrequited love. Heaven is the communion with perfect Life, perfect Truth, and perfect Love, God the Father, God the Son, and God the Holy Ghost to whom be all honor and glory forever and ever. Amen.

⋞ IN THE very nature of things, ethics and morality can exist only upon the condition of a veto. Bravery, for example, is possible only in a world in which a man may be a coward. Virtue is possible only in a world where a man may be vicious. Sacrifice is possible only in that order in which a man may be selfish. Love is possible only when it is possible not to love. Cold statues cannot love. It is the possibility of saying "No" which gives so much charm to the heart when it says "Yes." A victory may be celebrated only on those fields in which a battle may be lost. Hence, in the divine order of things, God made a world in which man and woman would rise to moral heights, not by that blind driving power which makes the sun rise each morning, but rather by the exercise of that freedom in which one may fight the good fight and enjoy the spoils of victory, for no one shall be crowned unless he has struggled.

◄§ ORIGINAL SIN alone can explain the almost contradictory character of human nature which makes a man aspire to higher things and at the same time succumb to the baser. The only reason we ever seek the nobler things of God is that we once possessed them; we seek because once we found.

◄§ LOVE tends to become like the one loved; in fact, it even wishes to become one with the one loved. God loved unworthy man. He willed to become one with him, and that was the Incarnation. One night there went out over the stillness of an evening breeze, out over the white chalked hills of Bethlehem, a cry, a gentle cry. The sea did not hear the cry, for the sea was filled with its own voice. The earth did not hear the cry, for the earth slept. The great men of the earth did not hear the cry, for they could not understand how a child could be greater than a man. The Kings of the earth did not hear the cry, for they could not fathom how a King could be born in a stable. There were only two classes of men who heard the cry that night: Shepherds and Wise Men. Shepherds: those who know they know nothing. Wise Men: those who know they do not know everything.

✧§ WILL eternity be anything like what I have seen or what I have heard, or what I can imagine? No, eternity will be nothing like anything I have seen, heard or imagined. Listen to the voice of God: "That eye hath not seen, nor ear heard, neither hath it entered into the heart of man, what things God hath prepared for them that love him." (I CORINTHIANS 2:9.)

✧§ PHILOSOPHICAL systems, scientific constructions, and slogans leave the heart of man cold. Even a theory about love means little as long as it remains a theory. But let love become personal in some one and then it pulls at every heart-string in the world. There is the secret of the appeal of the Incarnation. Love became Incarnate and dwelt amongst us. Since that day hearts that have known what the Incarnation means can never content themselves with any system which asks us to adore the cosmos. Man never has loved, never will love anything he cannot get his arms around, and the cosmos is too big and too bulky. That is why the Immense God became a Babe in order that we might encircle Him in our arms.

✧§ OH! tell me, how can hands bless that are nailed fast? How can lips that are bruised and parched with desolation preach the tidings of Divine Love? How can feet that are dug with steel go after souls that are lost? They cannot. And if we are to undo the harm that we have done, we must make our way up the penitential slope of Calvary, up to the chalice of all common miseries, and cast ourselves at the foot of the Cross. We must kneel there at the foot of that Pulpit of Love and confess that when we stabbed His Heart, it was our own we slew. But, oh, it is such a difficult thing to climb up the hill of Calvary! It is such a humiliating thing to be seen at the foot of the Cross! It is such a painful thing to be with one in pain and to be seen with one condemned by the world! It is such a hard thing to kneel at the foot of the Cross, and admit that one is wrong. *It is hard; but it is harder to hang there!*

৺ SAINTS fear hell but never deny it; great sinners deny hell but never fear it.

৺ CHRIST, then, must have meant what He said when He declared that His Church would endure even to the consummation of the world.

There emerges, then, from her history one great and wonderful lesson, and it is this: Christ rose from the dead, not because He is man, but because He is God. The Church rises from the sepulchre in which violent hands or passing errors would inter her, not because she is human, but because she is Divine. Nothing can rise from the dead except Divinity. The world should profit by experience and give up expecting the Church to die. If a bell had been tolled on a thousand different occasions and the funeral never took place, men would soon begin to regard the funeral as a joke. So it is with the Church. The notice of her execution has been posted, but the execution has never taken place. Science killed her, and still she was there; History interred her, but still she was alive. Modernism slew her, but still she lived.

৺ GOD is more anxious to save us than we are to save ourselves. There is a story told to the effect that one day Our Blessed Lord appeared to Saint Jerome, saying to him, "Jerome, what will you give Me?" Jerome answered, "I will give you my writings," to which Our Lord replied that it was not enough. "Then," said Jerome, "what shall I give you? My life of penance and mortification?" But the answer was, "Even that is not enough!" "What have I left to give Thee?" cried Jerome. Our Blessed Lord answered, "Jerome, you can give Me your sins."

৺ MAKE this experiment whether you believe in God or not. At your first opportunity stop in a Catholic Church for a visit. You need not believe as we Catholics do, that Our Lord is really and truly present in the tabernacle. But just sit there for an hour, and within that hour you will experience a surpassing peace the like of which you never before enjoyed in your life.

◄§ IT IS a common remark that nature is indifferent to our griefs. A nation may be dying of famine, yet the sun starts and plays upon the stricken fields. Brother may rise up against brother in a war which turns poppy fields into Haceldamas of blood; yet a bird, safe from the fire and shell, chants its little song of peace. Hearts may be broken by the loss of a friend; yet a rainbow leaps with joy across the heavens, making a terrible contrast between its smile and the agony it shines upon. But the sun refused to shine on the crucifixion! The light that rules the day, probably for the first and last time in history, was snuffed out like a candle when, according to every human calculation, it should have continued to shine. The reason was that the crowning crime of man, the killing of nature's Lord, could not pass without a protest from nature itself. If the soul of God were in darkness, so should be the sun which He had made.

◄§ IF we knew ourselves better, we would be more forgiving of others. The harder we are on ourselves, the easier we will be on others; the man who has never learned to obey knows not how to command; and the man who has never disciplined himself knows not how to be merciful.

◄§ IT IS not hatred that is wrong; it is hating the wrong thing that is wrong. It is not anger that is wrong, it is being angry at the wrong thing that is wrong. Tell me your enemy and I will tell you what you are. Tell me your hatred and I will tell you your character.

Do you hate religion? Then your conscience bothers you. Do

you hate capitalists? Then you are avaricious and you want to be a capitalist. Do you hate the laborer? Then you are selfish and a snob. Do you hate sin? Then you love God. Do you hate your hate, your selfishness, your quick temper, your wickedness? Then you are a good soul, for "If any man come to me . . . and hate not his own life he cannot be my disciple." (LUKE 14:26.)

⨳ ONE day a woman went to the saintly Father John Vianny, the Curé of Ars, in France, and said: "My husband has not been to the sacraments or to Mass for years. He has been unfaithful, wicked, and unjust. He has just fallen from a bridge and was drowned—a double death of body and soul." The Curé answered: "Madam, there is a short distance between the bridge and the water, and it is that distance which forbids you to judge."

⨳ LUST is an inordinate love of the pleasures of the flesh. The important word here is inordinate for it was Almighty God Himself who associated pleasure with the flesh. He attached pleasure to eating in order that we might not be remiss in nourishing and preserving our individual lives; He associated pleasure with the marital act in order that husband and wife might not be remiss in their social obligations to propagate mankind and raise children for the Kingdom of God. The pleasure becomes sinful at that point where, instead of using it as means, we begin to use it as an end. To eat for the sake of eating is a sin, because eating is a means to an end, which is health. Lust, in like manner, is selfishness or perverted love.

⨳ PRIDE is an inordinate love of one's own excellence, either of body or mind or the unlawful pleasure we derive from thinking we have no superiors. Pride being swollen egoism, it erects the human soul into a separate center of originativeness apart from God, exaggerates its own impor-

76

tance, and becomes a world in and for itself. All other sins are evil deeds, but pride insinuates itself even unto good works to destroy and slay them. For that reason Sacred Scriptures says: "Pride goeth before destruction."

◄§ NEGLECT the body and the muscles stiffen; neglect the mind and imbecility comes; neglect the soul and ruin follows. Just as physical life is the sum of the forces which resist death, so the spiritual life is to some extent the sum of the forces which resist evil. Neglect to take an antidote for a poison in the body, and we die by our neglect. Neglect to take precaution against sin, and we die the death merely because of neglect.

Heaven is a city on a hill, hence we cannot coast into it; we have to climb. Those who are too lazy to mount can miss its capture as well as the evil who refuse to seek it. Let no one think he can be totally indifferent to God in this life and suddenly develop a capacity for Him at the moment of death.

◄§ IN THE Christian order it is not the important who are essential, not those who do great things who are really great. A king is no nobler in the sight of God than a peasant. The head of government with millions of troops at his command is no more precious in the sight of God than a paralysed child. The former has greater opportunities for evil, but like the widow in the Temple, if the child fulfills its task of resignation to the will of God more than the dictator fulfills his task of procuring social justice for the glory of God, then the child is greater. "God is no respecter of persons."

◄§ MAY we never die too soon! This does not mean not dying young; it means not dying with our appointed tasks undone. It is indeed a curious fact that no one ever thinks of Our Lord as dying too young! That is because He finished His Father's business. But no matter how old we are when we die, we always feel there is something more to be done.

Why do we feel that way, if it is not because we did not do well the tasks assigned to us. Our task may not be great; it may be only to add one stone to the Temple of God. But whatever it is, do each tiny little act in union with your Saviour who died on the Cross and you will *finish* your life. Then you will never die too young!

&s COVETOUSNESS is an inordinate love of the things of this world. It becomes inordinate if one is not guided by a reasonable end, such as a suitable provision for one's family, or the future, or if one is too solicitous in amassing wealth, or too parsimonious in dispensing it.

The sin of covetousness includes therefore both the intention one has in acquiring the goods of this world and the manner of acquiring them. It is not the love of an excessive sum which makes it wrong, but an inordinate love of any sum.

Simply because a man has a great fortune, it does not follow that he is a covetous man. A child with a few pennies might possibly be more covetous. Material things are lawful and necessary in order to enable us to live according to our station in life, to mitigate suffering, to advance the Kingdom of God and to save our souls.

&s WITH a loud cry, so powerful that it freed His soul from His flesh and bore witness to the fact that He was giving up His life and not having it taken away, He said in farewell: "Father, into Thy Hands I commend My Spirit."

It rang out over the darkness and lost itself in the furthermost ends of the earth. The world has made all kinds of noise since to drown it out.

Men have busied themselves with nothing to shut out hearing it; but through the fog and darkness of cities, and the silence of the night that awful cry rings within the hearing of every heart who does not force himself to forget, and as we listen to it we learn two lessons:

1. The more ties we have to earth the harder will it be for us to die.

2. We were never meant to be perfectly satisfied here below.

    ✎§ T H E money we spend in the excesses of bodily hunger and thirst will do us no good on the last day; but the poor whom we have assisted by our restraint and mortification will stand up as so many advocates before the bar of Divine Justice, and will plead for mercy on our souls, even though they once were heavily laden with sin.

once admit a purpose in life,
and each and every act which tends toward that point,
bears the unmistakable stamp of joyfulness and cheer

ONCE admit a purpose in life, and each
and every act which tends toward that point, bears the unmistakable stamp of joyfulness and cheer. The Christian has his
fixed goal, namely, to make his life more and more Christ-like.
His own nature is like a block of marble, and his will is the
chisel. He looks out upon his model, Christ, and with the sharp
points of his mortifying chisel, cuts away from his nature great
huge chunks of cold selfishness, and then by finer and more delicate touches makes the great model appear forthwith, until
finally only the brush of a hand is needed to give it its polished
finish. There is no man living who has this Christian ideal who
believes that repeated acts of faith, hope and charity, prudence,
justice, fortitude and love are tainted with what the modern
mind would call monotony. Each new conquest of self is a new
thrill, for each repeated act brings closer and closer that love
we fall just short of in all love, eternal union with Our Lord
and Saviour.

✳ THE world's greatest need is some one who will understand that there is no greater conquest than victory over oneself; some one who will realize that real worth is achieved not so much by activity, as by silence; who will seek first the Kingdom of God and His justice, and put into actual practice the law that it is only by dying to the life of the body that we ever live to the life of the spirit; who will brave the taunts of a Good Friday to win the joy of an Easter Sunday; who will, like a lightning flash, burn away the bonds of feeble interest which tie down our energies to the world; who with a fearless voice, like John the Baptist, will arouse our enfeebled nature out of the sleek dream of unheroic repose; some one who will gain victories not by stepping down from the Cross and compromising with the world, but who will suffer in order to conquer the world. In a word, what we need are saints, for saints are the truly great men.

✳ MEN look forward to the possession of power— they finally get it, and still they are unhappy. Men crave wealth —they have a hundred times more than they need, and still they want more, and their wanting it makes them unhappy. Even the loss of the least of it robs them of joy, as the plucking of a single hair from a head that is full of it, gives pain. Nothing ever comes up to our expectations.

Well, why is it? The reason is that in looking forward to the things of this world, we use our imagination, which, as a faculty of the soul is spiritual, and therefore capable of imagining infinite things.

✳ YOU may have heard a great deal about a certain person, about his mannerisms, about his severity, about his rigorous life. You only know *about* him, but you do not *know* him. With this meager knowledge you frankly avow that you do not care for him. After spending five minutes in his company, your whole feeling has completely changed. Knowledge changed your whole outlook on him, and converted hate into the beginning of love. In much the same way that the prejudice of Nathaniel against Our Blessed Lord was changed by just two sentences from Our Lord's lips, sentences which swept away prejudice, so it is with the soul of a great man before Our Lord. At a distance Our Lord seems to be a harsh Master bearing a crown of thorns upon His head and a cross upon His shoulders. We fear lest having Him we must have naught else beside. Then one day we meet Our Lord, perhaps in sorrow or in pain, and we pass five minutes with Him, and our whole outlook on Him completely changes.

✳ SANCTITY is not giving up the world. It is exchanging the world. It is a continuation of that sublime transaction of the Incarnation in which Christ said to man: "You give Me your humanity, I will give you My Divinity. You give Me your time, I will give you My eternity. You give Me your bonds, I will give you My omnipotence. You give Me your slavery, I will give you My freedom. You give Me your death, I will give you My life. You give Me your nothingness, I will give you My all." And the consoling thought throughout this whole transforming process is that it does not require much time to make us saints; it requires only much love.

✳ THE world today needs some right of sanctuary, wherein poor tired hearts might be free from the curious inquisitiveness of the press; it needs some haven wherein we might be alone with ourselves and our God, free from the publication of our sins to the world; some place of shelter from the curious eyes of those who, rather than bind up our wounds, delight in our outpourings; some solitary harbor where we might escape those who, though they ask us to reveal, never stop to heal; some sanctuary where our sins would not be told to the world, nor allowed to fester unseen within our heart; some sanctuary from which we could pour out our souls to the God of love for the purposes of peace and pardon. And the world has such a sanctuary which respects the inviolability of the human person, a sanctuary wherein a soul may cast its lot, not upon inquiring men, but upon a forgiving God, and that is the Sacrament of Penance, or Confession.

❋ EVERY search for truth, every scientific enquiry, every piece of historical research, every painstaking microscopic study of a biological field, every search for new stars and distant planets, is really a search for God, for every quest for knowledge is a quest for Truth.

❋ CONFESSION demands a confessor: a man who will look kindly on the denying Peters, speak words of forgiveness to penitent Magdalenes, breathe words of comradeship to betraying Judases; a man who will utter a cry of forgiveness as if from a cross to all those who would malign him or his office; a man with intensity of love for his work and with universality of love for his penitents; a man endowed with the wisdom that comes with training, one in whom the Church has laid the wisdom garnered from twenty centuries' experience with souls; a man signed with the sign and sealed with the seal of Christ, and therefore, one who can love without loving; a man of discretion, that is, with a mind strange to curiosity, vanity, and fear; and, finally, a man with a heart like an immense well into which sins like stones may be dropped, but a well so deep that no sound comes back from those depths to an ear which might be bent to hear.

❋ CONFESSION is different from psychoanalysis not only in what is told, but also in the reason for telling it. The reason for telling things in psychoanalysis is to acquire mental ease; but the reason for telling sins in the confessional is to acquire pardon. Psychoanalysis is on the plane of medicine; man is treated in the same manner as an animal might be treated. But confession is on the plane of justice; man is treated as a sinner. Psychoanalysis tells things for the sake of sublimation, but not for the sake of purgation. It is not enough to diagnose a disease: it must be also cured, but there is no cure for a guilty conscience except pardon. The sinner must in some way be brought to Calvary and made to see the personal equation between himself and the sufferings of Christ, and this is done only in the confessional.

✻ A SAINT is one who has learned to spiritualize and sacramentalize and ennoble everything in the world, and make of it a prayer. No occupation is too base for such spiritualization, nor is any suffering too hard for such ennobling. It is only those who have not this highly developed sense that let the opportunities of daily life pass by without either making of them a prayer, or drawing from them a divine lesson. Centuries ago according to a story perhaps apocryphal, in the streets of Florence there stood a beautiful piece of Carrara marble that had been cut and hacked and ruined by some cheap artist. Other mediocre artists passed it by, and bemoaned that it should have been so ruined. One day Michelangelo passed it by, asked that it be brought to his studio. He there applied to it his chisel, his genius, and his inspiration. He drew out of it the immortal statue of David. The lesson contained herein is that there is nothing so base or low that it cannot be reconquered, that there is no duty however menial that cannot be retrieved for sanctity, and that there is nothing that is cast down that cannot be lifted up.

✻ IT IS easy to be an atheist, and to say the world does not require a God, just as it is easy to be a pantheist, and say that the world is God; but it is thrilling to walk between those two abysses and hold that God is in the world, but not of it—and such is the Incarnation. It would be easy to fall into the extreme of the Stoics, and say that pain is the law of life, or to fall into the equally stupid extreme of saying pleasure is the law of life, but it is romantic to escape the pitfalls and hold that pain is the prelude to life—and such is the lesson of Easter.

✳ I PLEAD for a Christmas in which the Babe is not an Orphan, but a Child of Mary; I plead for a religion which breathes respect for Motherhood, and vibrates with a love for that Mother, above all mothers, who brought Our Saviour into the world. If there is any man or woman looking for a test as to what constitutes the divine religion on this earth, let him apply the same test he would to the judgment of a man. If you ever want to know the real qualities of a man, judge him not by his attitude to the world of commerce, his outlook on business, his kindness and his genteel manners, but judge him rather by his attitude to his own mother. If you want to know the quality of a religion, judge it exactly the same way, that is, not by the way it seeks to please men, but rather by the attitude that it bears to the Mother of Our Blessed Lord. If you find a religion which never speaks of that Woman who gave us our Redeemer; a religion which in its liturgy and its devotions, is silent about that most beautiful of women; and in its history has even broken her images and statues, then there certainly must be something wanting to the truth of that religion, and let me add, even to its humanity.

✳ IN MOMENTS of silence, men begin to seek God. The self-conscious spirit emerges from the flux of life and in contemplation and reflection finds itself dissatisfied with what it has, and hankers after what it has not. The soul begins to part company with animal desires, and begins at least a blundering search for the hiding place of that haunting presence which seems to speak to him from every burning bush. The embryonic instinct for heaven now cries out for its object, and as the vague sense of unexplained powers conditions it, reflection begins, and reflection means asking oneself the question, "Why am I here?" and finding the answer in the words of the penny catechism, "To know, love and serve God, in this world, and be happy with Him forever in the next."

✳ TO ASK that religion be free from dogma is like asking that a body be freed from its backbone, or that art be freed from shape and proportion, and that literature be freed from grammar. I know there are thousands of minds weak enough to succumb to the succulent abstraction of the sweet catchword: "I believe in religion, but not in theology," but it is only a catchword. Such a mind might just as well say, "I believe in chemicals, but not in chemistry," or, "I believe in health, but not in all the medical dogmas about digestion, vitamins, and assimilation." It is all as vain and as senseless as saying, "I want to be really scientific, but let us do away with laboratories and technique." An open mind is good—but if it's open all around . . . Well!

✲ T H E Church and the State belong to two distinct spheres and there may be, therefore, a true and loyal allegiance to both, for we are to "render unto Caesar the things that are Caesar's, and to God the things that are God's." As a matter of fact, only those who love the spiritual can ever love the natural. Full and loving service of the Church of Christ no more conflicts with the love of nation, than the love of the soul is at variance with the love of the body. The loves, paradoxical though they may seem, merge into unity, thanks to the charity of our Sovereign Head who loved His own country even to the point of weeping over its capital city, and shedding the salt tears of the first Christian Patriot. He Who reserved the first fruits of His message for the lost sheep of Israel was the same One Whose flame of charity embraced the whole world, and whose life was surrendered on the gibbet of a Cross for the redemption of all people, for all climes and all times.

✲ T R U E G R E A T N E S S resides in qualities of the heart, in charity, justice, peace, purity, love; it is the development of our inner life, the enriching of our minds, the strengthening of our wills, the purification of our hearts; and the people who are bearers of the deepest love, the holiest faith, and work most firmly under the inspiration of the Leader on the Cross— these are the true patriots of America! And these are the patriots the Church is striving to produce by reminding man

that he reaches his highest point of development when he con-
quers the forces of nature by his knowledge, and then in turn
is conquered by Christ the King, Who, in His turn, in His human nature, is subject to His Own Heavenly Father, and Who
will, at the end of time, deliver all things unto Him. True civilization is a recognition of the primacy of the spiritual: "All are
yours, you are Christ's and Christ is God's."

✳ Do not forget that there are not two kinds of
answers to prayer, but three: One is "Yes." Another is "No."
The third is "Wait."

✳ The Church is very modern, if modern means
serving the times in which we live, but she is not modern, if it
means believing that whatever is modern is true. The Church
is modern, if modern means that her members should change
their hats with the seasons, and even with the styles, but she is
not modern, if it means that every time a man changes his hat,
he should also change his head, or in an applied sense, that she
should change her idea of God every time psychology puts
on a new shirt, or physics a new coat.

She is modern, if modern means incorporating the new-found
wisdom of the present with the patrimony of the centuries, but
she is not modern, if it means sneering at the past as one might
sneer at a lady's age. She is modern, if modern means a passionate desire to know the truth, but she is not modern if it means
that truth changes with the calendar, and that what is true on
Friday is false on Saturday. The Church is modern if modern
means progress toward a fixed ideal, but she is not modern if
it means changing the ideal instead of attaining it.

✳ Our happiest times are those in which we for-
get ourselves, usually in being kind to someone else. That tiny
moment of self-abdication is an act of true humility: the man
who loses himself finds himself and finds his happiness.

✻ IT IS unfortunately true that totalitarian states can more readily appeal to sacrifice than some democracies, for having imbued their people with a diabolical mysticism and having infused them with a false fervor, they are ready to deny themselves for a future glory.

But when democracies lose the spirit of religion they have no fulcrum for self-sacrifice; once the Cross passes out of their vision selfishness enthrones itself. Then the plea for self-sacrifice becomes identified with persecution, Fascism, Communism, or what-have-you.

The preservation of America is conditioned upon discipline and self-sacrifice, but since these are inseparable from religion and morality, the future of America depends on Americans' attitude toward God and the Cross of His Divine Son.

✻ IT WAS NOT weakness which made Christ hang on the Cross; it was obedience to the law of sacrifice, of love. For how could He save us if He ever saved Himself?

✻ IF OUR AGE lacks any quality at all, it is what might be called teachableness, or what the Latins called docility. Minds today rely principally on what they have obtained by their own thought or reading. Some fancy they can find out truth entirely by themselves and disdain the idea that God might add to their knowledge by revelation. Others believe that Wisdom is synonymous with a smattering of facts about science, or the book of the month, or the new skull dug up in Peiping. Even university education has become so impregnated with the research of useless facts, that it forgets research is only a means to an end, which is the discovery of Truth. It is well to remember that Herod is what many of our universities would have called a man of research, for he inquired diligently where the Child was born. But the Wise Men understood education far better. They were men of research too, for they searched the skies—but they were humble enough to know that research was only an instrument, and so they followed their science of the stars until it brought them to the Wisdom who made the stars, Jesus Christ Our Lord.

✳ I T I S the winds and the winters which try the herbs, the flowers, and the trees, and only the strongest survive. So tribulation tries the soul, and in the strong it develops patience, and patience, in its turn, hope, and hope finally begets love.

✳ E V E R Y M A N is passionately fond of liberty, but there is one thing he craves even more, and without which existence and even liberty is painful, and that is happiness. It is one of the greatest of life's paradoxes that as much as man seeks to be free, he still wishes to be a slave: not a slave in the sense that his liberty is denied him, but in the sense that he yearns for something he can worship, something which will solicit his will, pull at his heartstrings, tempt his energies, and command his affections. He wants to be free to choose between the various kinds of happiness, but he does not want to be free from happiness. He wishes to be its slave.

There are two ways of responding to this soul hunger and this heart thirst. One is the way of the world, the other is the way of Christ. The difference between the two is that before we have the pleasures of the world they seem desirable and all that we need to make us happy. But after we have them, they are disappointing and sometimes even disgusting. The contrary is true of the pleasures of Christ. Before we have them they are hard, unattractive, and even repulsive. But after we have them they are satisfying, and all our heart could ever crave.

✳ C H R I S T I A N character is nothing more nor less than the reconciling of opposite virtues. In other words, a really great character is not just a brave man, for if a man were brave without being tender, he might very easily become cruel. Tenderness is what might be called the other wing to bravery. In like manner, majesty alone does not make character, for majesty without gentleness might very soon degenerate into pride. Love of Peace alone does not make character, for without the opposite virtue of courage, peacefulness could very easily slip into a spineless cowardice. Wisdom without simplicity makes a man proud; simplicity without wisdom makes a man a simpleton. A real character therefore does not possess a virtue on a given point on the circumference without, at the same time, possessing the complementary virtue which is diametrically opposed to it; for what is character, but the tension between opposites, the equilibrium between extremes.

✻ P A I N and suffering are from sin and selfishness, but sacrifice is not; it is from love. It is through want of love that pain arises. Suffering brings one to the door of the Temple; but love is the key that unlocks the door, and by transmuting pain into sacrifice prepares for the happiness of the everlasting dwellings.

Those who have themselves never felt hunger involuntarily through fasting, can little understand the legitimate demands of the poor, or the obligation to feed them in charity.

In like manner, those who never have experienced suffering, which can be a condition of love, cannot understand how Christian souls resign themselves to Someone Who first loved us.

✻ M A N has a higher destiny than he knows; but unlike all things below him, he attains it not by self-extinction but by a surrender of the baser part of him, that he may perfect that higher faculty which makes him really a man, a child of God, and an heir of the Kingdom of Heaven.

✻ S U F F E R I N G often removes a false sense of values. It makes this problem acute: Are we going forward according to the will of God and every law written in our nature, or are we going to stand alone saving our miserable selfish lives, and in the end lose them?

In great moments of tragedy, sorrow, and pain, we are often given sudden intuitive visions of the utter hollowness and emptiness of life apart from God.

Suffering always begets in us a longing for security; that is why, when the staff of the material upon which we lean pierces our hands, we toss it away and look for a new staff upon which to lean.

✳ WE DO NOT KNOW why God does not answer all our petitions, though He has told us that before we speak, He has already heard us.

St. James however suggests selfishness is one reason for unanswered prayer: "You covet and you do not have; you kill and envy, and cannot obtain. You quarrel and wrangle, and you do not have because you do not ask. You ask and do not receive, because you ask amiss, that you may spend it upon your passions." (JAMES 4:2, 3.)

Many a man in the United States is living with only one eye or one finger, simply because his parents gave him exactly what he wanted on the Fourth of July.

I am sure that God has never answered and never will answer a baldheaded man's prayer for hair; and a woman could pray from now until the crack of doom, but God would never take the wart off the end of her nose.

Think these reflections through and you will understand why not all prayers are answered. God is omnipotent. He can do all things except one thing: He cannot please everybody.

✳ AT CHRISTMAS when someone asks us what we want, do we not say, "You choose," knowing full well that his generosity will be greater than our daring?

Why not begin prayer that way, trusting in Him because He knows what is best. That is why petition is not the essence of prayer: Trust, for one thing, underlies it.

✳ PRAYER does not so much help our conduct as our conduct tests our prayers. If we think right, we will live right.

The greatest stupidity ever uttered was "It makes no difference what you believe, but only how you act." Nonsense! We act on our beliefs; if they are wrong, we live wrong. Prayer then comes before conduct.

Live with the God of love, in prayer and you will act lovingly towards your neighbor. Think with the Christ on His Cross, and you will be charitable to your neighbor.

Your actions tell whether you ever pray—not your ears. Prayer is not getting something; it is becoming something.

✻ J U D A S still roams the world in the person of all those who were baptized to Christ and called to be one with Him, but who have fallen away from their high destiny by "selling out."

In the catalogue of Fascism, Nazism, and Communism you will find those who in their youth were signed with the sign of the Cross, sealed with the seal of salvation, and then like Judas bargained away their Christian heritage for thirty pieces of silver from the coffers of a transitory political power.

✻ W E C A N N O T M E E T a cross in our respective walks of life but that He already took it at the foot of Pilate's temple and made it the badge of His glory and the symbol of a Christian.

We cannot have feet tired and worn from the service of others but that His own were calloused from going about doing good and nailed to a Cross for having been too good.

We cannot have the sorrow of losing friends or a mother but that He Himself already felt the rent in His Own Heart, as He left a friend to a mother on the gibbet of a Cross.

If then He is in us, we shall overcome the world as He did, by the same love.

✻ T H E most sublime act in the history of Christ was His *Death*. Death is always important for it seals a destiny. Any dying man is a scene. Any dying scene is a sacred place.

That is why the great literature of the past which has touched on the emotions surrounding death has never passed out of date. But of all deaths in the record of man, none was more important than the Death of Christ. Everyone else who was ever born into the world, came into it to *live;* Our Lord came into it to *die.* Death was a stumbling block to the life of Socrates, but it was the crown to the life of Christ. He Himself told us that He came "to give his life a redemption for many"; that no one could take away His Life; but He would lay it down of Himself.

✳ M A S S is to us the crowning act of Christian worship. A pulpit in which the words of Our Lord are repeated does not unite us to Him; a choir in which sweet sentiments are sung brings us no closer to His Cross than to His garments. A temple without an altar of sacrifice is non-existent among primitive peoples, and is meaningless among Christians. And so in the Catholic Church the altar, and not the pulpit or the choir or the organ, is the center of worship, for there is re-enacted the memorial of His Passion. Its value does not depend on him who says it, or on him who hears it; it depends on Him who is the One High Priest and Victim, Jesus Christ Our Lord. With Him we are united, in spite of our nothingness; in a certain sense, we lose our individuality for the time being; we unite our intellect and our will, our heart and our soul, our body and our blood, so intimately with Christ, that the Heavenly Father sees not so much *us* with our imperfection, but rather sees us *in Him,* the Beloved Son in whom He is well pleased.

✳ T H A T word "Forgive," which rang out from the Cross that day when sin rose to its full strength and then fell defeated by Love, did not die with its echo. Not long before that same merciful Saviour had taken means to prolong forgiveness through space and time, even to the consummation of the world. Gathering the nucleus of His Church round about Him, He said to His Apostles: "Whose sins you shall forgive, they are forgiven."

Somewhere in the world today then, the successors of the

Apostles have the power to forgive. It is not for us to ask: But how can man forgive sins?—for man cannot forgive sins. But God can forgive sins *through* man, for is not that the way God forgave His executioners on the cross, namely through the instrumentality of His human nature?

✳ COMMUNION is first of all the receiving of Divine Life, a life to which we are no more entitled than marble is entitled to blooming. It is a pure gift of an all-merciful God who so loved us that He willed to be united with us, not in the bonds of flesh, but in the ineffable bonds of the Spirit where love knows no satiety, but only rapture and joy.

✳ DO WE really understand the nature of love? Have we not sometimes, in great moments of affection for a little child, said in language which might vary from this, but which expresses the idea, "I love that child so much, I should just like to possess it within myself?" Why? Because all love craves for unity. In the natural order, God has given great pleasures to the unity of the flesh. But those are nothing compared to the pleasure of the unity of the spirit, when divinity passes out to humanity, and humanity to divinity—when our will goes to Him, and He comes to us, so that we cease to be men and begin to be children of God.

If there has ever been a moment in your life when a fine, noble affection made you feel as if you had been lifted into the third or the seventh heaven; if there has ever been a time in your life when a noble love of a fine human heart cast you into an ecstasy; if there has ever been a time when you have really loved a human heart—then, I ask you, think of what it must be to be united with the great Heart of Love! If the human heart in all of its fine, noble, Christian riches can so thrill, can so exalt, can make us so ecstatic, then what must be the great heart of Christ? Oh, if the spark is so bright, what must be the flame!

✳ IF OUR LIVES just "end," our friends will ask: "How much did he leave?" But if our life is "finished" our friends will ask: "How much did he take with him?" A finished life is not measured by years but by deeds; not by the time spent in the vineyard, but by the work done. In a short time a man may fulfill many years; even those who come at the eleventh hour may finish their lives; even those who come to God like the thief at the last breath, may finish their lives in the Kingdom of God. Not for them the sad word of regret: "Too late, O ancient Beauty, have I loved Thee."

✳ THE Crucifixion was not meant to be an inspirational drama, but a pattern act on which to model our lives. We are not meant to sit and watch the Cross as something done and ended like the life of Socrates. *What was done on Calvary avails for us only in the degree that we repeat it in our own lives.*

The Mass makes this possible, for at the renewal of Calvary on our altars we are not on-lookers but sharers in Redemption, and there it is that we "finish" our work. He has told us: "And I, if I be lifted up from the earth, will draw all things to myself." He finished His work when He was lifted up on the Cross; we finish ours when we permit Him to draw us unto Himself in the Mass.

EATH is not the end of all. The cold clod falling upon the grave does not mark *finis* to the history of a man. The way he has lived in this life determines how he shall live in the next. If he has sought God during life, death will be like the opening of a cage, enabling him to use his wings to fly to the arms of the divine Beloved. If he has fled from God during life, death will be the beginning of an eternal flight away from Life and Truth and Love—and that is hell.

Before the throne of God, whence we came on our earthly novitiate, we must one day go back to render an account of our stewardship. There will not be a human creature who, when the last sheaf is garnered, will not be found either to have accepted or rejected the divine gift of Redemption, and in accepting or rejecting it to have signed the warrant of his eternal destiny.

◄§ THE world is full of those who suffer unjustly and who through no fault of their own bear the "slings and arrows of outrageous fortune." What should be our attitude to those who speak untruly of us, who malign our good names, who steal our reputations, and who sneer at our acts of kindness?

The answer is to be found in the first word from the Cross: *forgive.* If there was ever anyone who had a right to protest against injustice it was He Who is Divine Justice; if ever there was anyone who was entitled to reproach those who dug His hands and feet with steel, it was Our Lord on the Cross.

◄§ ONE reason for a long life is penance. Time is given us not just to accumulate that which we cannot take with us, but to make reparation for our sins.

That is why in the parable of the fig tree which had not borne fruit for three years and which the owner wished to cut down because it "cumbereth the ground" the dresser of the vineyard said: "Let it alone this year also, until I dig about it, and dung it. And if happily it bear fruit." (LUKE 13:6–9.)

So the Lord is with the wicked. He gives them another month, another year of life that they may dig their soul with penance and dung it with mortification, and happily save their souls.

◄§ THE cruelest master is the man who never learned to obey, and the severest judge is the man who never examines his own conscience. The man who is conscious of his need of absolution is the one who is most likely to be indulgent to others.

◄§ YOU and I often ask God for many favors which are never granted. We can imagine the thief on the right during his life asking God for many favors, and very especially for wealth which was probably not granted. On the other hand, though God does not always grant our material favors, there is one prayer He always grants.

There is a favor that you and I can ask of God this very moment, if we had the courage to do it, and that favor would be granted before the day is over. That prayer which God has never refused and will never refuse is the prayer for suffering. Ask Him to send you a cross and you will receive it!

But why does He not always answer our prayers for an increase in salary, for larger commissions, for more money? Why did He not answer the prayer of the thief on the left to be taken down from the cross, and why did He answer the prayer of the thief on the right to forgive his sins?

Because material favors draw us away from Him, but the cross always draws us to Him. And God does not want the world to have us!

He wants us Himself because He died for us!

◄§ T H E real test of the Christian is not how much he loves his friends, but how much he loves his enemies.

◄§ T H E faithful loyal wife whose husband is snatched from her by death, the mother whose son refuses to visit her and bless her declining days with filial affection, the friend who has sacrificed all only to be betrayed by one for whom he gave all—all these experience the keenest and bitterest of all human sufferings: the pangs of unrequited love. Such victims can and really do die of a broken heart.

But what is this love for another human being, compared to the love of God for man? The affection a human heart bears for another lessens as it multiplies the objects of its love, just as a river loses its fullness the more it divides itself into little streams.

But with God there is no decrease of love with the increase of objects loved, any more than a voice loses its strength because a thousand ears hear it.

◄§ W E C A N hammer iron, because it is material; we can melt ice, because we can warm it with our fires; we can break twigs, because we can get them into our hands; but we cannot crucify Faith, we cannot melt Hope, we cannot break Charity, and we cannot murder Justice, because all these things are spiritual and therefore beyond the power of enslavement.

In a higher sense, the soul of every man is the last and impregnable fortress of character. As long as he wills to keep his spirit his own, no one can take it away, even though they take his life.

◆§ FREEDOM has lost its value for the modern world. It understands freedom too often as the right to do whatever you please, or the absence of constraint. This is not freedom but license, and very often anarchy.

Freedom means not the right to do what you *please*, but the right to do what we *should* in order to attain the highest and noblest ends of our nature.

◆§ THE basic struggle today is not between individualism and collectivism, free enterprise and socialism, democracy and dictatorship. These are only the superficial manifestations of a deeper struggle which is moral and spiritual and involves above all else whether man shall exist for the state, or the state for man, and whether freedom is of the spirit or a concession of a materialized society. It has not been given to every age in history to see the issue as clearly as it has been given to our own, for we have a double incentive to work for the peace and prosperity of the world: the first is the Gospel in its fullness, the second is the communism of Soviet Russia. The first teaches us that happiness comes from living rightly; the second, that misery comes from acting wrongly.

◆§ IN *self-discipline you "give up" nothing.* You merely "exchange." You find that you can get along without an excess of drink, but you cannot give up peace of mind or union with God, so you "exchange" one for another. "What exchange shall a man give for his soul?" (MATTHEW 16:26.)

◆§ LIBERALISM is a dangerous term to use simply because the modern mind never makes a distinction. If liberalism means a system which believes in progress toward freedom as the *right* to do whatever man *ought*, then liberalism is to be encouraged. If liberalism means a progressive repudiation of law and truth in the sense that freedom means the *right* to do whatever man *pleases*, then it is to be condemned. In the latter sense, the liberal is opposed to the reactionary though both have something in common; they never see permanence and change together. They take one to the exclusion of the other. The reactionary seizes upon permanency to the exclusion of change, and the liberal upon change to the exclusion of permanency. The reactionary wants things to remain as they are; the liberal wants change though he is little concerned with direction. The reactionary wants the clock but no time; the liberal wants the time but no clock. The reactionary believes in staying where he is, though he never inquires whether or not he has a right to be there; the liberal, on the contrary, never knows where he is going, he is only sure he is on his way.

◆§ THE modern mind resents any reference to the Devil. The fact is, however, that, though contemporary atheism has not convinced us there is no God, it has convinced us that there is a devil. When man forgets he has a soul he also forgets that there is a competition for it between the forces of good and evil. Those who penetrate the surface of things more deeply than others have seen that if there is no devil, then all the evil in the world must be attributed to human nature, and no member of the human race wants to believe his species is that diabolical.

THE best presentation . . . for those inclined to deny either evil or the demonic is the brilliant work of Denis de Rougemont, *The Devil's Share*, which he introduces with the suggestion that the knowledge of true danger may cure us of false fears. Meeting immediately the difficulty that Satan, though a myth, has personality, he answers: "The Devil *is* a myth, hence he exists and continues to be active. A myth is a story which describes and illustrates in dramatic form certain deep structures of reality."

 THE only place in the world where communism works is in a convent, for there the basis of having everything in common is that no one wants anything. Communism has not worked in Moscow, but it does work in a monastery.

 GOD will not allow unrighteousness to become eternal. Revolution, disintegration, chaos must be reminders that our thinking has been wrong, our dreams have been unholy. Moral truth is vindicated by the ruin that follows when it has been repudiated. The chaos of our times is the strongest negative argument that could ever be advanced for Christianity. Catastrophe becomes a testimony to God's power in a meaningless world, but by it God brings a meaningless existence to nought. The disintegration following an abandonment of God thus becomes a triumph of meaning, a reaffirmation of purpose. Adversity is the expression of God's condemnation of evil, the registering of Divine Judgment. As hell is not sin, but the effect of sin, so these disordered times are not sin, but the wages of sin. Catastrophe reveals that evil is self-defeating; we cannot turn from God without hurting ourselves.

 NEVER BEFORE in history has there been such a strong argument for the need of Christianity, for men are now discovering that their misery and their woes, their wars and their revolutions increase in direct ratio and proportion to the neglect of Christianity. Christians realize that a moment of crisis is not a time of despair, but of opportunity. The more we can anticipate the doom, the more we can avoid it. Once we recognize we are under Divine Wrath, we become eligible for Divine Mercy. It was because of famine the prodigal said: "I will arise, and will go to my father . . ." (LUKE 15:18.) The very disciplines of God create hope. The thief on the right came to God by a crucifixion. The Christian finds a basis for optimism in the most thorough-going pessimism, for his Easter is within three days of Good Friday.

ᴥ§ J E W S, Protestants and Catholics alike, and all men of good will, are realizing that the world is serving their souls with an awful summons—the summons to heroic efforts at spiritualization. An alliance among Jews, Protestants and Catholics is not necessary to fight against an *external* enemy, for our "wrestling is not against flesh and blood; but against principalities and powers, against the rulers of the world of this darkness, against the spirits of wickedness in the high places." (EPHESIANS 6:12.) We desire unity of religion but not when purchased at the cost of the unity of the truth. But we plead for a unity of religious peoples, wherein each marches separately according to the light of his conscience, but strikes together for the moral betterment of the world; a unity through prayer, not hate. If Satan has his fellow travelers, then why should not God and His Divine Son? The Roman sergeant who built a temple for the Jews was a fellow traveler with them in their belief in God. The woman at Tyre and Sidon became a fellow traveler of Christ. The forces of evil are united; the forces of good are divided. We may not be able to meet in the same pew—would to God we could—but we can meet on our *knees.*

ᴥ§ S A I N T S love sinners, not because they both have vice in common, but because the saint loves the possible virtue of the sinner. The Son of God became the Son of Man because He loved man.

⊷§ THE Catholic Church is sometimes praised for its opposition to communism. This compliment is deserved, for the Church is the only solid moral force in the world that has been consistently opposed to the new barbarism. The Church foresaw the evils of totalitarianism and condemned each in turn. The Church condemned Fascism in the Encyclical *Non Abiamo Bisogno* which was written in Italian because Fascism was a national phenomenon; it condemned Nazism in the German language in the Encyclical *Mit Brennender Sorge* because Nazism was a racial phenomenon. It condemned communism in the universal language of Latin in the Encyclical *Divini Redemptoris,* because communism is an international phenomenon. Communism in its turn has concentrated its attacks principally upon the Church, for the instinct of communism is infallible when it comes to knowing its enemy. It wastes no time on small fry; it has no delusions about the opposition. It knows that Christ not only claims to be Divine, but is Divine. Its persecution of the Church is indirect praise—it pays the beautiful tribute of hostility. If it ignored the Church, if it directed no arrows against our shields, then would the Church know that its faith had faltered and its fires had gone out, and its salt had lost its savor.

⊷§ JUDGE the Catholic Church not by those who barely live by its spirit, but by the example of those who live closest to it.

⊷§ THE communion of men one with another is a consummation devoutly to be wished, but it can never be achieved on a compulsory basis, or by the exterior organization of society, which impoverishes human personality and negates the spiritual in man. The rebirth of a new order cannot start with the denial of man, but with his reaffirmation as made to the Divine Image. No better start can be made than with the Christian doctrine that a man is more precious than the universe, that the universe exists for him, that society can use some human functions, but never at the cost of absorption, and that even in his evil moments man is worth addressing in the second person singular, as Our Lord did the thief in that beautiful affirmation of democracy on the cross: "This day *thou* shalt be with Me in Paradise."

&§ T H E Communist philosopher Engels defined liberty as "necessity." A stone is free when it obeys the law of gravitation and falls to the ground when released from the hand. Man is free according to the Communist view because he knows that he must act according to the laws of the dictator. When a man knows what he must do and does it, then he is free. Thus article 125 of the Soviet Constitution grants the citizens the right of freedom of press and speech and assembly *on condition* they are used to support the Communist system. This means that unless citizens use the press and speech and assembly to further communism, they thereby forfeit the rights. Communism supplied one defect of the liberal theory of freedom, by offering a purpose which is social, but it made this purpose so absolute as to destroy completely freedom of choice. This it did by absorbing personality into the class which is the essence of communism.

&§ P E O P L E living in dirt hardly ever realize how dirty dirt is. Those who live in sin hardly understand the horror of sin. The one peculiar and terrifying thing about sin is, the more experience you have with it, the less you know about it. You become so identified with it, that you know neither the depths to which you have sunk nor the heights from which you have fallen.

&§ L I B E R T Y is something more than an economic phenomenon as the disciples of free enterprise contend; liberty is more than a political phenomenon, as a tyrannical dictatorship claims; it is even more than the separation of right from responsibility as historical liberalism contended; it is something more than the separation of responsibilities from rights as communism contends; it is something else than free thought and something more than dictated thought. Historical liberalism was not the birth of liberty, and Communist dictatorship is not its discovery. Freedom had its roots in man's spiritual nature, before there was ever a liberal, a democrat, a Fascist, a Communist or a Nazi. Freedom does not arise out of any social organization or any constitution or any party, but out of the soul of man.

&§ THE basic defect of communism is the inescapable fact of death. Recently a work written on the subject of Communist philosophy had a brief chapter entitled "The Communist Attitude toward Death," and it contained nothing of the philosophy of communism, but only an excerpt from Gorky about how science was trying to master death. Practice bears this out, for all Red funerals are glorifications of the collectivity. The perfect symbol of its philosophy is the cadaver of Lenin with its periodical injections of embalming fluid to give it the semblance of permanence.

Death is the great unsolved problem of communism, because despite all the dictatorial attempts to absorb men into collectivity, the final breath individualizes and personalizes and individuates. For a time the Communist may feel he is like fruit on the tree of the classless society, in which all hang together as tree clings to skin, and skin to pulp, and pulp to seed, so he clings to the party, the party to the politburo and the politburo to the dictator. But he must remember that a day comes when the fruit falls from the tree; the pulp may become the prey of birds, but at the core of all is a seed which prepares for another life, sans party, sans politburo, sans dictator—an immortal soul.

&§ THE great fallacy of modern education is the assumption that the reason there is evil in the world is because there is ignorance, and that if we pour more facts in the minds of the young we will make them better. If this were true, we should be the most virtuous people in the history of the world, because we are the best educated.

⋖§ COMMUNISM should not be met by vituperation, namecalling and personal hate. Hate is like a seed—it grows. By hating Communists we advance communism, for communism grows in discord just as disease thrives in dirt. As Manzoni wrote: "Few things so corrupt a people as the habit of hate." Only a spurious distinction between individual and social morality has made possible the appeal to hate in the struggle of nations. Pius XII in his Christmas Message of 1940 declared that one of the first victories to be won is "victory over hate which is today dividing the nations." Communism is an ideology and as such is intrinsically wicked, but Communists are persons, made to the image and likeness of God and, therefore, should be subjects of our kindness and charity, that we may prove ourselves worthy children of the Heavenly Father. There is no erring soul that cannot attain to the treasures of Redemption. It is precisely out of love for the sinner that the sin is hated. "The very fact that we hate in our brother his fault and the absence of good is because of our love of our brother." Not even the violence of communism abrogates, but rather renders more imperative, the Christian law.

⋖§ THE Christian point of view is to see ourselves as part of a guilty world. In fact, the more innocent we are, the more we are to feel that guilt, because then we better recognize our oneness with our fellow men. Our Lord was innocent, but He took on Himself the sins of the world. How can we be bearers of one another's burdens, as Scripture enjoins, unless it be by seeing that when we touch the circle of humanity at any one point, we touch humanity? Our mission is not exclusively to protest against the evils of our materialistic civilization, not merely to challenge its assumptions, or even diminish its severities— but in some way to see ourselves as citizens of a guilty world. Guilt is social as well as personal, because man is formed for fellowship. There is no thought more salutary in the present crisis than the recognition that much of it is due to our own unfulfilled Christian duties.

❧ A NATION always gets the kind of politicians it deserves. When our moral standards are different, our legislation will be different. As long as the decent people refuse to believe that morality must manifest itself in every sphere of human activity, including the political, they will not meet the challenge of Marxism.

❧ THE modern world has no cement to bind together personal morals and the morals of political and economic life. If a time ever comes when the religious Jews, Protestants and Catholics have to suffer under a totalitarian state denying them the right to worship God according to the light of their conscience, it will be because for years they thought it made no difference what kind of people represented them in Congress, and because they never opposed the spiritual truth to the materialist lie. St. Paul said: "Woe is me if I preach not the Gospel," (I CORINTHIANS, 9:16) and woe unto us, if the believing element in our country does not allow its belief in God and morality to seep down into its action in the polling booths. The first effective campaign against communism is to wage war against our temptation to abandon the spiritual in the realm of the political. Nothing can do men of good will more harm than apparent compromises with parties that subscribe to antimoral and antidemocratic and anti-God forces. We must have the courage to detach our support from men who are doing evil. We must bear them no hatred, but we must break with them.

❧ THERE ARE seven ways in which Charity may be expressed spiritually:

> To instruct the ignorant.
> To counsel the doubtful.
> To admonish sinners.
> To bear wrongs patiently.

To forgive offences willingly.
To comfort the afflicted.
To pray for the living and the dead.

⇛ WHEN men and women reach a point where they are no longer interested in watching a seed that they have planted grow, or caring for its flower; when they are more concerned about increasing dollars in their bank account than obeying the primitive impulse to increase and multiply—then know ye that a night has dawned when a *thing* is more important than a *person*, and *Hic jacet* must be inscribed on the tombstone of democracy. Beyond and behind all the schemes and blueprints of politics and economics, there is nothing more fundamental to the revival of true democracy than the restoration of the family. In that circle shall our citizens learn that there is other wealth than paper wealth, paper money, paper stocks, paper joys, namely, the tingling, vibrating wealth of children, the unbreakable bond between husband and wife, the pledge of democracy and the future heirs of the Kingdom of Heaven.

⇛ THERE ARE two extremes to be avoided in discussing married love: one is the refusal to recognize sexual love, the other is the giving of primacy to sexual attraction. The first error was Victorian; the second is Freudian.

⇛ ALL irresponsibility brings in its train the desire to be possessed; either by music which excites him viscerally, or by alcohol, sleeping tablets and noise, all of which help him to escape the responsibility of conscience. Once men admit themselves determined by alien influences outside the moral law written in their hearts, they become raw material for a propaganda of repetition which submerges them in the divinized power of the anonymous. As responsibility implies religion, so irresponsibility implies anti-religion, as the new collectivism gives the depersonalized man an object of worship in place of God. Totalitarianism grows in direct ratio and proportion to the decline of responsibility in the individual.

≈§ SINCE the world has lost Christ, it may be that through Mary it will recover Him. When Our Blessed Lord was lost at the age of 12, it was the Blessed Mother who found Him. Now that He has been lost again, it may be through Mary that the world will recover Christ their Saviour. Another reason is that Divine Providence has committed to a woman the power of overcoming evil. In that first dread day when evil was introduced into the world, God spoke to the serpent in the Garden of Eden and said: "I shall put enmity between thee and the woman; between thy seed and her seed, and thou shalt lie in wait for her heel." (GENESIS 3:15.) In other words, evil shall have a progeny and a seed. Goodness too shall have a progeny and a seed. It will be through the power of the woman that evil will be overcome. We live now in an evil hour, for though goodness has its day, evil does have its hour. Our Blessed Lord said that much the night that Judas came into the garden: "This is your hour, the power of darkness." (LUKE 22:53.) All evil can do in that hour is to put out the lights of the world; but it can do that. If then we live in an evil hour how shall we overcome the spirit of Satan except by the power of that Woman to whom Almighty God has given the mandate to crush the head of the serpent?

≈§ EVERY PERSON is what he loves. Love becomes like unto that which it loves. If it loves heaven, it becomes heavenly; if it loves the carnal as a god, it becomes corruptible. The kind of immortality we have depends on the kind of loves we have. Putting it negatively, he who tells you what he does not love, also tells what he is. "*Amor pondus meum:* Love is my gravitation," said St. Augustine.

≈§ THE revelation of Fatima is a reminder that we live in a moral universe, that evil is self-defeating, that good is self-preserving; that the basic troubles of the world are not in politics or economics but in our hearts and our souls, and that spiritual regeneration is the condition of social amelioration. Soviet Russia is not the sole danger to the Western world; rather is it the despiritualization of the Western world to which Russia gave political form and social substance. World War II came according to Our Lady of Fatima because there was no amendment in the hearts and souls of men. The danger of World War III is precisely in this point, not just in the Communist International. The Western world is scandalized at the Soviet system, but this is basically because it sees its own individual atheism socialized and put into practice on almost a cosmic scale. The great issue at stake is not individualism or collectivism, because neither of these is of primary importance; it is not between free enterprise and socialism in the economic order, for neither of these matters tremendously; rather the struggle is for the human soul.

&s THE world is the way it is because each of us is the way we are. It is the special responsibility of the Christian to discern in two world wars in 21 years the judgment of God on the way we live. As long as the Christian thinks that there are only two directions he can take, "Right" or "Left," not only will he make no contribution to the world, but he will make the world worse by failing to recognize that additional to the horizontal plane of life, there is also the vertical which leads to God and where there are two more important directions of "inward" and "upward." Not by finding scapegoats, whether they be political parties or communism, will we escape the responsibility of bearing, as Christ did in Gethsemane, the burden of the world's guilt. The revelation of Fatima was a most poignant reminder to Christians that the so-called problem of Russia is the problem of Christians: that by prayer, penance and reparation, and not by war, abuse and attack will Russia join the society of freedom-loving nations.

&s WHEN God takes someone from us, it is always for a good reason. When the sheep have grazed and thinned the grass in the lower regions, the shepherd will take a little lamb in his arms, carry it up the mountain where the grass is green, lay it down, and soon the other sheep will follow. Every now and then Our Lord takes a lamb from the parched field of a family up to those Heavenly Green Pastures, that the rest of the family may keep their eyes on their true home and follow through.

◄§ As AMERICANS we cannot be unmindful of the relation of this country to the Woman to whom God gave the power of crushing the head of the serpent. The Council of Baltimore on December 8, 1846, consecrated the United States to the Immaculate Conception of Our Blessed Mother. It was only 8 years later that the Church defined Her Immaculate Conception. It was on December 8, 1941, the Feast of the Immaculate Conception, that the United States went to war with Japan. It was on May 13, 1945, Mother's Day, the day on which the entire Church celebrated Sodality Day of Our Lady, that the United States Government proclaimed a National Thanksgiving for V-E Day. It was on August 15, 1945, the Feast of the Assumption of Our Blessed Mother, that victory came to us in the war with Japan. It was the nineteenth of August, 1945, that the United States Government declared official V-J Day and this happened to be the anniversary of one of the appearances of Our Lady at Fatima. On September 1, 1945, the first Saturday of the month which Our Lady of Fatima asked should be consecrated to Her, General MacArthur accepted the surrender of Japan aboard the *Missouri*. It was on September 8, 1945, the Birthday of Our Lady, that the first American flag flew over Tokyo, and as it was unfurled General MacArthur said: "Let it wave in its full glory as a symbol of victory for the right."

SEX is one of the means God has instituted for the enrichment of personality. It is a basic principle of philosophy that there is nothing in the mind which was not previously in the senses. All our knowledge comes from the body. We have a body, St. Thomas tells us, because of the weakness of our intellect. Just as the enrichment of the mind comes from the body and its senses, so the enrichment of love comes through the body and its sex. As one can see a universe mirrored in a tear on a cheek, so in sex can be seen mirrored that wider world of love.

✳ To LOVE what is below the human, is degradation; to love what is human for the sake of the human, is mediocrity; to love the human for the sake of the Divine, is enriching; to love the Divine for its own sake is sanctity.

✳ M A N has his feet in the mud of the earth, his wings in the skies. He has sensations like the beasts and ideas like the angels, without being either pure beast or pure spirit. He is a mysterious composite of body and soul, with his body belonging to a soul, and his soul incomplete without the body. The true order is the subjection of body to soul and the whole personality to God. "It is all for you, and you for Christ, and Christ for God." (I Corinthians 3:23.) Man is the pontiff of the universe, the "bridge builder" between matter and spirit, suspended between one foundation on earth and the other in heaven. He is also, fundamentally, a being in *tension* with an anxiety of the kind felt by a sailor halfway up to a crow's nest on a stormy sea. His duty calls him to the nest above; his earth-bound character makes him fear falling from his ladder.

✳ W h e n love is limited to the satisfaction of egotistic desire, it becomes only a spent force, a fallen star. When it deliberately refuses to use the sparks which God gave it to enkindle other fires; when it digs wells, but never drains the water; when it learns to read, but never knows: then does love turn against itself, and because it desires only to enjoy its own life, it ends in hatred or mutual slaughter.

✳ L o v e that is only giving, ends in exhaustion; love that is only seeking, perishes in its selfishness. Love that is ever seeking to give and is ever defeated by receiving is the shadow of the Trinity on earth, and therefore a foretaste of heaven. Father, Mother, Child, three persons in the unity of human nature: such is the Triune law of Love in heaven and on earth. "No one can love without being born of God, and knowing God." (I John 4:7.) Love is an eternal mutual self-gift; the recovery in the flesh, or in the soul, or in heaven, of all that was given and surrendered. In love no fragment is lost.

✳ L o v e never grows old except to those who put its essence into that which grows old: the body. Like a precious liquid, love shares the lot of the container. If love is put in a vessel of clay, it is quickly absorbed and dried; if, like knowledge, it is placed in the mind, it grows through the years, becoming stronger, even as the body grows weaker. The more it is united with the spirit, the more immortal it becomes.

✳ F IDELITY in marriage implies much more than abstention from adultery. All religious ideals are positive, not negative. Husband and wife are pledges of eternal love. Their union in the flesh has a grace which prepares and qualifies both souls for the union with God. Salvation is nothing but wedlock with God. All those who have taken hold of Christ in marriage wear a "yoke that is sweet and a burden that is light." As yoke-mates of love, they pull together in the tilling of the field of the flesh, until there is finally revealed to them the full splendor of harvest in eternal union with God.

✳ O NE of the great joys of eternity will be seeing the correlation between all branches of knowledge, arts and sciences and the Word and Wisdom of God. But even now the dim glimpses we catch of that order make us see all human generation as the reflection of the eternal generation of the Word in the bosom of the Father.

✳ G OD gives to each man the divine life of grace, if he desires it. But He also wants man to be the channel of that Divine Life. If man refuses to give human life, God cannot give Divine Life. But whereas man can refuse to give human life, and therefore limits the creation of more souls, God Himself can never refuse to give the body of a child a soul. God obeys man and woman in their union, just as He obeys the priest at the moment of consecration. Even though the priest who consecrates be unworthy, God nevertheless descends onto the altar. However unworthy and illegal the union of man and woman, God does not refuse to give to the fruit of this union an immortal soul.

✳ A MOTHER is a double benefactor to humanity: its physical preserver, and its moral provider. Through life, and through the high personal qualities of her children, she is the universe's constant challenge to death, the messenger of cosmic plenitude and the bearer of eternal realities.

✳ A WOMAN is capable of more sustained sacrifice than man. Man is more apt to be the hero in one great, passionate outburst of courage. But a woman is heroic through the years, months, and even seconds of daily life, the very repetition of her toils giving them the semblance of the commonplace. Not only her days but her nights, not only her mind, but her body, must share in the Calvary of Mothering. She, therefore, has a greater understanding of redemption than man, for she comes closer to death in bringing forth life.

✳ THE first direct, human limitation of infant life in the history of Christianity took place in the village of Bethlehem through an Infant-Controller whose name was Herod. The prevention of infant life was simultaneously an attack upon Divinity in the person of God made man, Jesus Christ, Our Lord. No one strikes at birth who does not simultaneously strike at God, for birth is earth's reflection of the Son's eternal generation.

✳ MARRIAGE must end in the family, at least in intention if not in act; for only through the family does life escape exhaustion and weariness by discovering its duality to be trinity, by seeing its love continually reborn and reknown, by having its mutual self-giving transformed into receiving. Love thus defeats death, as it defeats exhaustion. It achieves a kind of immortality as self-renewal becomes self-preservation. God is eternal society; Three Persons in one Divine Nature. The family is human society; mutual self-giving which ends in self-perfection.

✳ THE greatest joys of life are purchased at the cost of some sacrifice. No one ever enjoys good reading, good music, or good art without a certain amount of study and effort. Neither can one enjoy love without a certain amount of self-denial. It is not that love by its nature demands suffering, for there is no suffering in Divine Love. But whenever love is imperfect, or whenever a body is associated with a soul, there must be suffering, for such is the cost of love's purification. One cannot grow from ignorance to love of poetry without discipline. Neither can one mount from one level of love to another without a certain amount of purification. The Blessed Virgin passed from one level of love, which was for her Divine Son, to the higher level of love for all whom He would redeem, by willing His Passion and Death at the Marriage Feast of Cana.

✳ THERE comes to every human, at one period or another, the discovery of his nothingness. The man who wanted a certain position eventually becomes dissatisfied with it, and wants something higher; he who has wealth does not have enough, not even with the first million. So in married love, there comes the crisis of not completely realizing the ideal. But this crisis of nothingness which comes to everyone, whether he is married or not, does not mean that life is to be mocked. *One has not hit the bottom of life, but only the bottom of one's ego.* One has not hit the bottom of his soul, but only of his instinct; not the bottom of his mind, but of his passions; not the bottom of his spirit, but of his sex. The aforementioned trials are merely so many contacts with reality which Almighty God sends into every life, for what we are describing here is common to every life. If life went on as a dream without the shock of disillusionment, who would ever attain his final goal with God and perfect happiness? The majority of men would rest in mediocrity; acorns would be content to be saplings; some children would never grow up and nothing would mature.

✳ THINK not that in order to "know life" you must "experience evil." Is a doctor wiser because he is prostrate with disease? Do we know cleanliness by living in sewers? Do we know education by experiencing stupidity? Do we know peace by fighting? Do we know the joys of vision by being blinded? Do you become a better pianist by hitting the wrong keys? You do not need to get drunk to know what drunkenness is.

✻ T H E fallacy of sex education is assuming that if children know the evil effects of certain acts, they will abstain from those acts. It is argued that if you knew there was typhoid fever in a house you would not go into that house. But what these educators forget is that the sex appeal is not at all like the typhoid fever appeal. No person has an urge to break down the doors of a typhoid patient, but the same cannot be said about sex. There is a sex impulse but there is no typhoid instinct.

Sex wisdom does not necessarily make one wise; it can make one desire the evil, particularly when we learn that the evil effects can be avoided. Sex Hygiene is not morality. Soap is not the same as virtue. Badness comes not from our ignorance of knowing, but from our perversity of doing.

That is why in our Catholic schools we train and discipline the will as well as inform the intellect, because we know that character is in our choices, not in our knowing. All of us already *know* enough to be good, even before we start to school. What we have to learn is how to *do better*.

✻ T H E R E is only one thing in the world that is definitely and absolutely your own, and that is your will. Health, power, possessions and honor can all be snatched from you, but your will is irrevocably your own, even in hell. Hence, nothing really matters in life, except what you do with your will.

there are as many kinds of crosses
as there are persons

OUR Lord deals separately with each soul. The crown of gold we want may have underneath it the crown of thorns, but the heroes who choose the crown of thorns often find that underneath it is the crown of gold. Even those that seem to be without a cross actually have one.

No one would have ever suspected that when Mary resigned herself to God's Will by accepting the honor of becoming the Mother of God, she would ever have to bear a cross. It would seem, too, that one who was preserved free from original sin should be dispensed from the penalties of that sin, such as pain. Yet this honor brought to her seven crosses and ended by making her the Queen of Martyrs.

There are, therefore, as many kinds of crosses as there are persons: crosses of grief and sorrow, crosses of want, crosses of abuse, crosses of wounded love and crosses of defeat.

⊷§ SICKNESS always has a Divine purpose. Our Blessed Lord said: "This sickness is not unto death, but for the glory of God: that the Son of God may be glorified by it." (JOHN 11:4.) Resignation to this particular kind of cross is one of the very highest forms of prayer.

⊷§ BECAUSE our crosses differ, soul will differ from soul in glory. We think too often that in Heaven there is going to be somewhat the same equality in social positions that we have here; that servants on earth will be servants in heaven; that the important people on earth will be the important people in heaven. This is not true.

God will take into account our crosses. He seemed to suggest that in the parable of Dives and Lazarus: "Son, remember that thou didst receive good things in thy lifetime, and likewise Lazarus evil things: but now he is comforted and thou art tormented." (LUKE 16:25.)

There will be a bright jewel of merit for those who suffer in this world. Because we live in a world where position is determined economically, we forget that in God's world the royalty are those who do His Will; Heaven will be a complete reversal of value of earth. The first shall be last and the last first, for God is no respecter of persons.

⊷§ IT IS typically American to feel that we are not doing anything unless we are doing something *big*. But from the Christian point of view, there is no one thing that is bigger than any other thing. The bigness comes from the way our wills utilize things. Hence mopping an office for the love of God is bigger than running the office for the love of money.

⊷§ IN WHAT does your life consist except two things? (1) Active duties. (2) Passive circumstances. The first is under your control; these do in God's name. The second is outside your control; these submit to in God's name. Consider only the present; leave the past to God's Justice, the future to His

Providence. Perfection of personality does not consist in knowing God's plan, but in submitting to it as it reveals itself in the circumstances of life.

⋖§ T H E reason most of us are what we are, mediocre Christians, "up" one day, "down" the next, is simply because we refuse to let God work on us. As crude marble we rebel against the hand of the sculptor; as unvarnished canvas we shrink from the oils and tints of the Heavenly Artists. We are so "fearful lest having Him we may have nought else beside," forgetful that if we have the fire of Love, why worry about the sparks, and if we have the perfect round, why trouble ourselves with the arc.

We always make the fatal mistake of thinking that it is what we do that matters, when really what matters is what we let God do to us. God sent the angel to Mary, not to ask her to do something, but to let something be done.

⋖§ I F Y O U have never before prayed to Mary, do so now. Can you not see that if Christ Himself willed to be physically formed in her for nine months and then be spiritually formed by her for thirty years, it is to her that we must go to learn how to have Christ formed in us? Only she who raised Christ can raise a Christian.

⋖§ B E C A U S E the "Hail Mary" is said many times in the course of a Rosary, do not think of it as a sterile repetition, because each time it is said in a different setting or scene as you meditate, for example, on such mysteries as the Birth of Our Lord, the Crucifixion, the Resurrection, etc. You never thought as a child, when you told your mother you loved her, that it had the same meaning as it did the last time you told her. Because the background of the affection changed, its affirmation was new. It is the same sun that rises each morning, but it makes a new day.

৵ IF YOU are unhappy, or sad, or despondent, it is basically for only one reason: you have refused to respond to Love's plea: "Come to me, all you that labour and are burdened, and I will refresh you. Take up my yoke upon you and learn of me, because I am meek, and humble of heart: and you shall find rest to your souls." (MATTHEW 11:28–29.)

৵ GIVE God a chance. The prolongation of His Incarnate Life in the Church is an offer, not a demand. It is a gift, not a bargain. You can never deserve it, but you can receive it. God is on the quest of your soul. Whether you will know peace depends on your own will. "If any man will do the will of him, he shall know of the doctrine, whether it be of God, or whether I speak of myself." (JOHN 7:17.)

৵ MANY married women who have deliberately spurned the "hour" of child-bearing are unhappy and frustrated. They never discovered the joys of marriage because they refused to surrender to the obligation of their state. In saving themselves, they lost themselves! It takes three to make love, not two: you and you and God. Without God people only succeed in bringing out the worst in each other. Lovers who have nothing else to do but love one another, soon find there is nothing else. Without a central loyalty life is unfinished.

৵ WHICH is right—the violence of Communism or the meekness of Christ? Communism says meekness is weakness. But that is because it does not understand the meaning of Christian meekness. Meekness is not cowardice; meekness is not an easy-going temperament, sluggish and hard to arouse; meekness is not a spineless passivity which allows everyone to walk over us. No! Meekness is self-possession. That is why the reward of meekness is possession.

A PERSON is merciful when he feels the sorrow and misery of another as if it were his own. Disliking misery and unhappiness, the merciful man seeks to dispel the misery of his neighbor just as much as he would if the misery were his own. That is why, whenever mercy is confronted not only with pain, but with sin and wrong-doing, it becomes forgiveness which not merely pardons, but even rebuilds into justice, repentance, and love.

MARRIAGE releases the flesh from its individual selfishness for the service of the family; the vow of chastity releases the flesh not only from the narrow and circumscribed family where there can still be selfishness, but also for the service of that family which embraces all humanity. That is why the Church asks those who consecrate themselves to the redemption of the world to take a vow and to surrender all selfishness, that they may belong to no one family and yet belong to all.

SOME years ago when the Cloister of a Carmelite convent was broken by a Cardinal and opened to the public, a good Carmelite nun was showing a visiting priest through the convent. From the roof of it one could look over a valley, and on to an opposite hill where there stood a large and beautiful home that seemed to stand as a symbol for all that was sweet and beautiful and lovely in life.

Recalling the economic poverty of this poor nun, the visitor said to her, "Sister, just suppose that before you entered Carmel, you could have lived in that home. Suppose that you could have had all the wealth, refinement, and opportunities for worldly enjoyment that such a home would give you. Would you have left that house to have become a poor Carmelite?" And she answered, "Father, that *is* my house!"

TO ALL you who mourn, He has said: "Blessed are you, for you shall be comforted." You have had your fast with Christ, now you shall have His feast. He has saved much for you; He kept something back when He was on earth. He has reserved it for those who have wept.

And that thing which he has kept for eternity, which will make your life's crucifixion seem as naught, which will make your eternity a blissful ecstatic passionless passion of love, which will be the ending of all beatitudes and the crown of all living, that thing which He has guardedly treasured for eternity, and which will make heaven heaven, will be—His Smile!

 WE DO NOT PRAY in order that we may change God's Will; we pray rather to change our own.

 YOU cannot always depend on prayers to be answered the way you want them answered, but you can always depend on God.

God, the loving Father, often denies us those things which in the end would prove harmful to us. Every boy wants a revolver at four, and no father yet has ever granted that request. Why should we think God is less wise? Some day we will thank God not only for what He gave us, but also for that which He refused.

 OUR LORD never discoursed on equality: He spoke to the Samaritans, ate with publicans and sinners, and offered His life for *all* men.

 AM I continually boasting and considering myself superior to my neighbor, either because he is ignorant, or poor, or a member of a certain class or race? "And whosoever shall exalt himself shall be humbled, and he that humbles himself shall be exalted." (MATTHEW 23:12.)

"There is neither Jew nor Greek; there is neither slave nor freeman. . . . For you are all one in Christ Jesus." (GALATIANS 3:28.)

◦§ I T I s hard to understand why God should seemingly care so much for sinners; but does not a mother rejoice more at the recovery of her sick child, than at the continued health of the rest of the family? Did not the Prodigal Son get the fatted calf, while the one who stayed at home was not so much as given a goat?

◦§ T H E Mass is the perpetuation of the Sacrifice of Calvary with the same Priest, and the same Victim. The difference is that Calvary was a bloody sacrifice; the Mass is offered in an unbloody manner. Furthermore on the Cross Our Lord was alone; in the Mass we are with Him.

We offer ourselves in the Mass with Christ through bread and wine. In the early Church we would have brought these elements. Today we bring that which buys bread and wine. Hence the offertory collection.

We bring bread and wine because these two things most of all nature represent the substance of life. Wheat is, as it were, the very marrow of the ground, and the grapes its very blood; both give us the body and blood of life.

In bringing those two things, which give us life and nourish us, we are equivalently bringing ourselves to the Sacrifice of the Mass.

◦§ T H E R E I s only one reason for being critical, and that is to be constructive, just as the only reason for razing a house is to make one rise in its place. There is perhaps too much of the sceptic in the critic today, in the sense that his protests are rarely followed by reforms and his denunciations but seldom succeeded by enunciations. A need exists for a renewal of something implied in the word "appreciation," in the etymological sense, namely, an evaluation or a judging of things by their real worth. But the real worth implies a standard, and a standard of thinking cannot be the fashion, but what is true.

◦§ N O O N E has a right to talk on the subject of persecution unless he condemns it wherever he finds it, and irrespective of who is persecuted, whether it be a Jew, a Protestant, or a Catholic. Persecution is not essentially anti-Semitic, it is not essentially anti-Christian. It is anti-human.

⋅§ DISRESPECT for rational foundations is the general readiness of the modern mind to accept a statement because of the literary way in which it is couched, or because of the popularity of the one who says it, rather than for the reasons behind the statement. In this sense, it is unfortunate that some men who think poorly can write so well. Bergson has written a philosophy grounded on the assumption that the greater comes from the less, but he has so camouflaged that intellectual monstrosity with mellifluous French that he has been credited with being a great and original thinker. To some minds, of course, the startling will always appear to be the profound. It is easier to get the attention of the press when one says, as Ibsen did, that "two and two make five," than to be orthodox and say that two and two make four.

⋅§ THIS whole problem of the dignity of man was thought out years ago by Aristotle, who called man a microcosm of a little universe, because he contained the cosmos within himself. Man sums up the lower order of creation in a double way: first, physically, and secondly, mentally. Physically, he is made up of a combination of chemicals, vegetative processes, and animal activities; he is like matter, because he exists; like plants, because he lives; and like animals, because he feels. But he is above all these because he has his own peculiar perfection; namely, an intelligence, which enables him to know not only the phenomena of earth and the movements of the heavens, but the intelligibility of these phenomena in terms of causes and, in particular, in terms of the First Cause, God.

SCIENCE is but the reduction of multiplicity to the unity of thought, and just as there can never be science without a scientist, so neither can there be law and order in the cosmos unless it was made with law and order. The mind of man does not put law into the universe; it discovers it. If man discovers intelligibility there, some one must have put it there in making the cosmos intelligently. Thus the "very silence of the spheres" that frightened Pascal drove him on mentally until he found a Transcendent Source of Wisdom for that immanent order, which source is the Infinite God, to Whom be all honor and glory forever.

✻ AGNOSTICISM is an evil when it contends not only that an individual mind knows nothing, but also that no other mind knows anything. In this sense it is cowardly, because it runs away from the problems of life. Only about ten per cent of the people think for themselves. Columnists and head-line writers think for the greater per cent of the remainder. Those who are left are the agnostics, who think agnosticism is an answer to the riddle of life. Agnosticism is not an answer. It is not even a question.

✱ THERE are then three sources of vision in this universe, each different in kind and yet each the perfection of the other—the eye, the reason, and faith. One unlocks the vestibule of creation or the material universe; the second unlocks the sanctuary of creation or the world of causes and finalities in the natural order; the third unlocks the Holy of Holies or the world of Incarnation and Grace.

✱ MORALITY means a conscious relation between the nature of man and the goal of his being; and secondly, it entails an immanent principle of guidance in the work, which is conscience. The immanent law in creation below man is unconscious and necessary. Hence, an acorn works out its destiny naturally: it grows to be an oak. Man, however, is free to stunt his growth, and to choose another end than the efflorescence of his faculties in union with Perfect Love. If man chooses, he need not grow up to be an oak; he can remain a poor sapling or just a "poor sap."

✱ THERE is knowledge in both religion and science, but the will plays a part in religion that it does not play in science, and it is his will that makes a man morally courageous, and not his knowledge. Theoretically, there should be a balance between knowledge and love, which is seated in the will—as there is in the Trinity, where the Son and Holy Spirit are equal—but practically, this is not true. There is many a professor of theology who knows a great deal about theology but who dies a Doctor of Divinity and not a saint, and there is many a man who knows but little of theology and less of science but who dies full of the love of God.

128

✳ THE Church is not only more fundamental than Fundamentalism, but she is also more modern than Modernism, because she has a memory that dates back over twenty centuries; and therefore she knows that what the world calls modern is really very ancient—that is, its modernity is only a new label for an old error. Modernism has an appeal only to minds who do not know what is ancient, or perhaps antiquated. The Church is like an old schoolmaster who has been teaching generations and generations of pupils. She has seen each new generation make the same mistakes, fall into the same errors, cultivate the same poses, each believing it has hit upon something new. But she, with her memory, which is tradition, knows that they are making the same mistakes all over again, for in the wisdom born of the centuries she knows very well that what one generation calls modern the next generation will call unmodern. . . . Having constantly refused to espouse the passing, she has never become a widow, but ever remains a mother to guide her children and to keep them not modern but ultra-modern, not behind the times but behind the scenes, in order that from that vantage-point they may see the curtain ring down on each passing modern fad and fancy.

✳ TRADITION is not, as some believe, a heritage of the Dark Ages, something that cabins and confines thought; rather, it is a memory. A sense and an intellectual memory are indispensable conditions of all right thinking. We are under the necessity of going back to the storehouse of our mind for past impressions and thoughts in order to build up the present thought. What is true of the individual is true of society. Tradition is the memory of society and without that tradition society cannot think. "It is owing to tradition," says Pascal, "that the whole procession of men in the course of so many centuries may be considered as a single mind who always subsists and who learns continually."

✳ THE bad Catholic who gives no glory to God, and offends Him, is heading for eternal loss. The non-Catholic who gives glory to God, according to the light of his conscience, is in his way to be saved. It ill-behooves a Catholic to act like the elder son when the prodigal came home. God is more anxious to see all His sheep in "one fold" than we are.

✳ SCIENTIFIC PROGRESS is said to have shown the futility of old dogmas, and the microscope is said to have revealed the inanities of theology.

For the mediaevalist, on the contrary, dogmas are no more subject to change than the multiplication table. Two and two make four for the thirteenth century as well as for the twentieth, and a dogma like that of the Incarnation is as true for the twentieth as it is for the thirteenth century. Dogmas are above space and time because they are not sentimental appreciations of a sentimentalist, but intellectual truths of an intellect. Neither is theology a mere science of comparative religions. St. Thomas teaches that theology is the queen of sciences, that "it surpasses all sciences in its principles, its object, its certitude, and its end." In theology everything possesses its own objective value; it is true in itself, apart from our appreciation of it. Its dogmas are not barriers to thought. They are no more confining for a mind than plan, contour, and choice of colors are confining for an artist. No great artist ever complained about the exigencies of dogma. A dogma is for the artist what the multiplication table is for the mathematician, or the logarithms are for the calculist, or the law of gravitation is for the physicist.

✳ THE Last Judgment finds its best expression in the central door of the Cathedral of Notre Dame of Paris. Christ is seated in His Majesty showing the wounds of His hands; beside Him is the cross with which He has conquered death, and round about Him are the Blessed Virgin and angels. In a lower panel angels are going forth to the four corners of the earth and the utmost bounds of them with trumpets summoning the dead to rise to judgment. The just are signed with the Tau, the cross, and are placed on the right; the unjust are placed on the left and bound with ropes to be cast into utter darkness.

✻ THERE IS a parallel between the Fall and the Redemption of man. Four elements contributed to the Fall: a disobedient man, Adam; a proud woman, Eve; a tree; and the fruit of the tree. Four elements contributed to our redemption: An obedient God-man, Jesus Christ; a humble woman, the Virgin Mary; a tree, the Cross; and the fruit of the Tree, Christ and the Eucharist. As the human race fell through a woman it was fitting that it should be redeemed through a woman. Mary is more than a mere accident in the reparation of the human race, and is represented as something more, namely, as the Mother of God.

✻ TO WORK truly for the good of society, one must be carried away by enthusiasm for something outside society. Humanism of itself is insufficient. Detachment from the individual can be accomplished by attachment to society, but detachment from society can be accomplished only by attachment to God. For this reason there never was enunciated a principle better destined to affect social disinterestedness than that of Him Who said: "Seek ye first the Kingdom of God and His justice and all these things will be added unto you."

✻ IT IS a strange paradox, but a true one, nevertheless, that man only becomes most human when he becomes most divine, because he has been destined from all eternity to be conformable to the image of the Son of God. Any form of Humanism, therefore, which denies the necessity of grace, and attempts to perfect man without it, is asking man to grow without an environment in which to grow. To remain on the level of the purely human, and to hold up the ideal of "decorum," is to permit man to expand horizontally, in the direction of the human, but not vertically, in the direction of the divine. Humanism allows for the spreading out of man on the plane of nature, but not for his being lifted up on the plane of grace, and elevation is far more important than expansion. Deny the order of grace, the realm of the Fatherhood of God, and what environment has humanity to grow in except poor weak humanity like himself? Since the soul is spiritual, man needs the environment not only of humanity, which belongs to the realm of his body, but that of spirit, which belongs to his soul, and it is only by entering into harmony with that great environment that he attains the end of his creation.

✻ I T is a tenet of the Catholic philosophy of charity that the lessening of the ills of mankind and the diminution of the traces of disease are not ends in themselves, but rather means to an end. In other words, philanthropy is not absolute in its end but sacramental. In the strict sense of the term, there are seven sacraments—material things used as means of spiritual sanctification. In the broad sense of the term, everything in the world is a sacrament, for everything in the world can be made a means of leading us on to Christ and hastening the reign of Christ.

✻ A R E the schools and universities throughout the country that ignore God really educating the young men and women entrusted to their care? Would we say that a man was a learned mathematician if he did not know the first principles of Euclid? Would we say that a man was a skilled littérateur if he did not know the meaning of words? Would we say that a man was a profound physicist if he did not know the first principles of light, sound, and heat? Can we say that a man is truly educated who is ignorant of the first principles of life and truth and love—which is God?

✻ T H E immorality of birth control is not a matter of authority but of common sense. It is too often said that birth control is wrong because the Catholic Church says it is wrong. No, birth control is wrong because reason says it is wrong; it is the misuse and abuse of certain faculties that God has given to mankind. But because the Church alone today upholds reason, that which reason condemns is identified with what the

Church condemns, and forgetting the profound rationalism that inspires her, men babble about her autocratic authority.

✳ WHEN God willed to become Man, He had to decide on the time of His coming, the country in which He would be born, the city in which He would be raised, the people, the race, the political and economic systems which would surround Him, the language He would speak, and the psychological attitudes with which He would come in contact as the Lord of History and the Saviour of the World.

All these details would depend entirely on one factor: the woman who would be His Mother. To choose a mother is to choose a social position, a language, a city, an environment, a crisis, and a destiny.

His Mother was not like ours, whom we accepted as something historically fixed, which we could not change; He was born of a Mother whom He chose before He was born. It is the only instance in history where both the Son willed the Mother, and the Mother willed the Son. And this is what the Creed means when it says, "born of the Virgin Mary." She was called by God as Aaron was, and Our Lord was born not just of her flesh, but by her consent.

✳ IN EACH CHILD God whispers a new secret to the world; adds a new dimension of immortality to creation; and makes the clinging hearts of husband and wife feel a little freer, as they look into that strange and mutual hope which has come to them from God.

✳ THIS special purity of (Mary's) we call the Immaculate Conception. It is not the Virgin Birth. The word "immaculate" is taken from two Latin words meaning "not stained." "Conception" means that, at the first moment of her conception, the Blessed Mother in the womb of her mother, St. Anne, and in virtue of the anticipated merits of the Redemption of her Son, was preserved free from the stains of original sin.

I never could see why anyone in this day and age should object to the Immaculate Conception; all modern pagans believe that they are immaculately conceived. If there is no original sin, then everyone is immaculately conceived. Why do they shrink from allowing to Mary what they attribute to themselves? The doctrine of Original Sin and the Immaculate Conception are mutually exclusive. If Mary alone is THE Immaculate Conception, then the rest of us must have Original Sin.

The Immaculate Conception does not imply that Mary needed no Redemption. She needed it as much as you and I do. She was redeemed in advance, by way of prevention, in both body and soul, in the first instant of conception. We receive the fruits of redemption in our soul at Baptism. The whole human race needs redemption. But Mary was desolidarized and separated from that sin-laden humanity as a result of the merits of Our Lord's Cross being offered to her at the moment of her conception. If we exempted her from the need of redemption, we would also have to exempt her from membership in humanity. The Immaculate Conception, therefore, in no way implies that she needed no redemption. She did! Mary is the first effect of redemption, in the sense that it was applied to her at the moment of her conception and to us in another and diminished fashion only after our birth.

✻ T H E beauty of this universe is that practically all gifts are conditioned by freedom. . . . The one word in the English language which proves the close connection between gifts and freedom is: "Thanks." As Chesterton said: "If man were not free, he could never say, 'Thank you for the mustard.'"

✻ T R U E L O V E always imposes restrictions on itself —for the sake of others—whether it be the saint who detaches himself from the world in order more readily to adhere to Christ, or the husband who detaches himself from former acquaintances to belong more readily to the spouse of his choice. True love, by its nature, is uncompromising; it is the freeing of self from selfishness and egotism. Real love uses freedom to attach itself unchangeably to another. St. Augustine has said: "Love God, and then do whatever you please." By this he meant that, if you love God, you will never do anything to wound Him. In married love, likewise, there is perfect freedom, and yet one limitation which preserves that love, and that is the refusal to hurt the beloved.

✳ An interesting insight into love is this—that, to just the extent that we reject love, we lose our gifts. No refugee from Russia sends a gift back to a Dictator; God's gifts, too, are dependent on our love. Adam and Eve could have passed on to posterity extraordinary gifts of body and soul, had they but loved. They were not forced to love; they were not asked to say, "I love," because words can be empty; they were merely asked to make an act of choice between what is God's and what is not God's, between the choices symbolized in the alternatives of the garden and the tree. If they had had no freedom, they would have turned to God as the sunflower does to the sun; but, being free, they could reject the whole for the part, the garden for the tree, the future joy for the immediate pleasure. The result was that mankind lost those gifts which God would have passed on to it, had it only been true in love.

✳ The mystery of the Incarnation is very simply that of God's asking a woman to freely give Him a human nature. In so many words, through the Angel, He was saying: "Will you make Me a man?" As from the first Adam came the first Eve, so now, in the rebirth of man's dignity, the new Adam will come from the new Eve. And in Mary's free consent we have the only human nature which was ever born in perfect liberty.

The story of this rebirth of freedom is told in the Gospel of St. Luke (1:26–35).

✳ The greatest act of freedom the world has ever known is the reversal of that free act which the Head of humanity performed in paradise when he chose non-God against God. It was the moment in which that unfortunate choice was reversed, when God in His Mercy willed to remake man and to give him a fresh start in a new birth of freedom under GOD. God could have made a perfect man to start humanity out of dust as He had done in the beginning. He could have made the new man start the new humanity from nothing, as He had done in making the world. And He could have done it without consulting humanity, but this would have been the invasion of human privilege. God would not take a man out of the world of freedom without the free act of a free being. God's way with man is not dictatorship, but cooperation. If He would redeem humanity, it would be with human consent, and not against it. God could destroy evil but only at the cost of human freedom, and that would be too high a price to pay for the destruction of dictatorship on earth—to have a dictator in Heaven.

❋ IN MARY ALONE, a Child waited not on nature, but on her acceptance of the Divine Will. All she had to say was Fiat, and she conceived. This is what all birth would have been without sin—a matter of human wills uniting themselves with the Divine Will and, through the union of bodies, sharing in the creation of new life through the usual processes of human generation. The Virgin Birth is, therefore, synonymous with Birth in Freedom.

❋ IF MARY were only the Mother of another man, then she could not also be our mother, because the ties of the flesh are too exclusive. Flesh allows only one mother. The step between a mother and a stepmother is long, and few there are who can make it. But Spirit allows another mother. Since Mary is the Mother of God, then she can be the Mother of everyone whom Christ redeemed.

❋ A CATHOLIC boy from a parochial school was telling a University professor who lived next door about the

Blessed Mother. The professor scoffed at the boy, saying: "But there is no difference between her and my mother." The boy answered: "That's what you say, but there's a heck of a lot of difference between the sons."

That is the answer. It is because Our Lord is so different from other sons that we set His Mother apart from all mothers. Because He had an Eternal Generation in the bosom of the Father as the Son of God, and a temporal generation in the womb of Mary as the Son of Man, His coming created a new set of relationships. She is not a private person; all other mothers are. We did not make her different; we found her different. We did not choose Mary; He did.

✳ AS OUR LOVE does not start with Mary, so neither does it stop with Mary. Mary is a window through which our humanity first catches a glimpse of Divinity on earth. Or perhaps she is more like a magnifying glass, that intensifies our love of her Son, and makes our prayers more bright and burning.

God, Who made the sun, also made the moon. The moon does not take away from the brilliance of the sun. The moon would be only a burnt-out cinder floating in the immensity of space, were it not for the sun. All its light is reflected from the sun. The Blessed Mother reflects her Divine Son; without Him, she is nothing. With Him, she is the Mother of Men. On dark nights we are grateful for the moon; when we see it shining, we know there must be a sun. So in this dark night of the world when men turn their backs on Him Who is the Light of the World, we look to Mary to guide their feet while we await the sunrise.

✳ THE philanthropists who give millions to erect art museums, libraries, and playgrounds out of purely humanitarian reasons will not further their eternal salvation as much as the poor widow who gives a nickel to a poor man on the street because in his need she sees the poverty of Christ.

✳ O N E of the most beautiful lessons in the world emerges from the Annunciation, namely, the vocation of woman to supreme religious values. Mary is here recapturing woman's vocation from the beginning, namely, to be to humanity the bearer of the Divine. Every mother is this when she gives birth to a child, for the soul of every child is infused by God. She thus becomes a co-worker with Divinity; she bears what God alone can give. As the priest in the order of Redemption, at the moment of Consecration, brings the crucified Saviour to the altar, so the mother in the order of creation brings the spirit which issues from the Hand of God to the cradle of earth. With such thoughts in mind, Leon Bloy once said: "The more a woman is holy, the more she becomes a woman."

✳ E V E R Y L A W, physical or moral, has its penalties. If I disobey the law of health, nature penalizes me with sickness. If I disobey the moral law, I cannot eternally hope to escape its consequences as though I had not violated it.

✳ V I R G I N I T Y and maternity are not so irreconcilable as it would seem. Every virgin yearns to become a mother, either physically or spiritually, for unless she creates, mothers, nurses, and fosters life, her heart is as uneasy and awkward as a giant ship in shallow waters. She has the vocation of generating life, either in the flesh or in the spirit through conversion. There is nothing in professional life which necessarily hardens a woman. If such a woman does become hardened, it is because she is denied those specifically creative God-like functions without which she cannot be happy.

On the other hand, every wife and mother strives for spiritual virginity in that she would like to take back what she has given, that she might offer it all over again, only this time more deeply, more piously, more divinely. There is something incomplete about virginity, something ungiven, unsurrendered, kept back. There is something lost in all motherhood: something given, something taken—and something irrecoverable.

But in the Woman there was realized physically and spiritually what every woman desires physically.

✳ O BEDIENCE in the home is the foundation of obedience in the commonwealth, for in each instance, conscience submits to a trustee of God's authority. If it be true that the world has lost its respect for authority, it is only because it lost it first in the home. By a peculiar paradox, as the home loses its authority, the authority of the State becomes tyrannical. Some moderns would swell their ego into infinity; but at Nazareth Infinity stoops down to earth to shrink into the obedience of a child.

✳ L OVE in its nature is an Ascension in Christ and an Assumption in Mary. So closely are Love and the Assumption related that a few years ago the writer, when instructing a Chinese lady, found that the one truth in Christianity which was easiest for her to believe was the Assumption. She personally knew a saintly soul who lived on a mat in the woods, whom thousands of people visited to receive her blessing. One day, according to the belief of all who knew the saint, she was "assumed" into heaven. The explanation the convert from Confucianism gave was: "Her love was so great that her body followed her soul." One thing is certain: The Assumption is easy to understand if one loves God deeply, but it is hard to understand if one loves not.

✳ L OVE is to a great extent a stranger on earth; it finds momentary satisfactions in human hearts, but it soon becomes restless. It was born of the Infinite and can never be satisfied with anything less. In a certain sense, God spoiled us for any other love except Himself, because He made us out of His Divine Love.

✻ THE major problem of the world is the restoration of the image of man. Every time a child is born into the world, there is a restoration of the human image, but only from the physical point of view. The surcease from the tragedy can come only from the restoration of the spiritual image of man, as a creature made to the image and likeness of God and destined one day, through the human will in cooperation with God's grace, to become a child of God and an heir of the Kingdom of Heaven. The image of man that was first ruined in the revolt against God in Eden was restored when the Woman brought forth a Man—a perfect man without sin, but a man personally united with God. He is the pattern of the new race of men, who would be called Christians. If the image of man was restored through a Woman, in the beginning, then shall not the Woman again be summoned by the Mercy of God, to recall us once again to that original pattern?

This would seem to be the reason for the frequent revelations of the Blessed Mother in modern times at Salette, Lourdes, and Fatima.

✻ WE SHOULD *never let a day pass without doing three small mortifications,* for example, not taking that extra cigarette or that second lump of sugar. Thus do we possess ourselves instead of being possessed by things. When these mortifications are done in the name of Our Lord, they become a source of great merit as well.

pleasure is the bait God uses to induce creatures
to fulfill their heavenly infused instincts

A MAN teaches a woman pleasure; a woman teaches a man continence. Man is the raging torrent of the cascading river; woman is the bank which keeps it within limits. Pleasure is the bait God uses to induce creatures to fulfill their heavenly infused instincts—pleasure in eating, for the sake of the preservation of the individual—pleasure in mating, for the sake of the preservation of the species. But God puts a limit to each to prevent the riotous overflow. One is satiety, which comes from nature itself and limits the pleasure of eating; the other is the woman who rarely confuses the pleasure of mating with the sanctity of marriage.

⁘ THE human heart is torn between a sense of emptiness and a need of being filled, like the waterpots of Cana. The emptiness comes from the fact that we are human. The power of filling belongs only to Him Who ordered the waterpots filled. Lest any heart should fail in being filled, Mary's last valedictory is: "Whatsoever He shall say to you, that do ye." The heart has a need of emptying and a need of being filled. The power of emptying is human—emptying in the love of others—the power of filling belongs only to God. Hence all perfect love must end on the note: "Not my will, but Thine be done, O Lord!"

&§ CONSECRATED virginity is the highest form of sacral or sacrificial love; it seeks nothing for itself, but only the will of the beloved. Pagans reverenced virginity, but they regarded it as almost the exclusive power of woman, for purity was seen only in its mechanical and physical effects. Christianity, on the contrary, looks upon virginity as a surrender of sex and of human love for God.

&§ THE problem of a woman is whether certain God-given qualities, which are specifically hers, are given adequate and full expression. These qualities are principally devotion, sacrifice, and love. They need not necessarily be expressed in a family, nor even in a convent. They can find an outlet in the social world, in the care of the sick, the poor, the ignorant—in the seven corporal works of mercy.

&§ THE unalterable fact is that no woman is happy unless she has someone for whom she can sacrifice herself—not in a servile way, but in the way of love. Added to the devotedness is her love of creativeness. A man is afraid of dying, but a woman is afraid of not living. Life to a man is personal; life to a woman is otherness. She thinks less in terms of perpetuation of self and more in terms of perpetuation of others—so much so, that in her devotedness she is willing to sacrifice herself for others. To the extent that a career gives her no opportunity for either, she becomes defeminized. If these qualities cannot be given an outlet in a home and a family, they must nevertheless find other substitutions in works of charity, in the defense of virtuous living, and in the defense of right, as other Claudias enlighten their political husbands. Then woman's work as a money earner becomes a mere prelude and a condition for the display of equity, which is her greatest glory.

&§ SOME *motives for self-discipline are:* To obtain peace of soul; to atone for one's sins; to obtain some favor or grace; to live a life more intimately with God; to conform oneself to Christ-suffering; to make reparation for the sins of others.

&§ IT IS objected that there is much repetition in the Rosary because the Lord's Prayer and the Hail Mary are said so often; therefore it is monotonous. That reminds me of a woman who came to see me one evening after instructions. She said, "I would never become a Catholic. You say the same words in the Rosary over and over again, and anyone who repeats the same words is never sincere. I would never believe anyone who repeated his words, and neither would God." I asked her who the man was with her. She said he was her fiance. I asked: "Does he love you?" "Certainly, he does." "But how do you know?" "He told me." "What did he say?" "He said: 'I love you.'" "When did he tell you last?" "About an hour ago." "Did he tell you before?" "Yes, last night." "What did he say?" "'I love you'" "But never before?" "He tells me every night." I said: "Do not believe him. He is repeating; he is not sincere."

&§ SELF-DISCIPLINE *requires patience.* Since we do not acquire evil habits in a day, we will not break them in a day. The abuses of years may take years to rectify. "If any man will come after me, let him deny himself, and take up his cross daily, and follow me." (LUKE 9:23.)

&§ THE Rosary is the best therapy for distraught, unhappy, fearful, and frustrated souls, precisely because it involves the simultaneous use of three powers: the physical, the

143

vocal, and the spiritual, and in that order. The fingers, touching the beads, are reminded that these little counters are to be used for prayer. This is the physical suggestion of prayer. The lips move in unison with the fingers. This is a second or vocal suggestion of prayer. The Church, a wise psychologist, insists that the lips move while saying the Rosary, because She knows that the external rhythm of the body can create a rhythm of the soul. If the fingers and the lips keep at it, the spiritual will soon follow, and the prayer will eventually end in the heart.

꙳ T H E more one descends to humility, the deeper becomes the faith. The Blessed Mother thanked her Divine Son because He had looked on her lowliness. The world starts with what is big, the spirit begins with the little, aye, with the trivial! The faith of the simple can surpass that of the learned, because the intellectual often ignore those humble means to devotion, such as medals, pilgrimages, statues, and Rosaries. As the rich, in their snobbery, sneer at the poor, so the intelligentsia, in their sophistication, jeer at the lowly. One of the last acts of Our Lord was to wash the feet of His Disciples, after which He told them that out of such humiliation true greatness is born.

꙳ T H E Rosary is the book of the blind, where souls see and there enact the greatest drama of love the world has ever known; it is the book of the simple, which initiates them into mysteries and knowledge more satisfying than the education of other men; it is the book of the aged, whose eyes close upon the shadow of this world, and open on the substance of the next. The power of the Rosary is beyond description.

꙳ T H E Rosary relates the Christian life to that of Mary. The three great mysteries of the Rosary—the Joyful, the Sorrowful, and the Glorious—are the brief description of earthly life contained in the Creed: birth, struggle, and victory. Joyful: "Born of the Virgin Mary." Sorrowful: "Suffered under Pontius Pilate, was crucified, died and was buried." Glorious: "The third day He arose again from the dead, sitteth at the right hand of God, the Father Almighty." The Christian life is inseparable from the joys of birth and youth, the struggles of maturity against the passions and evil, and finally, the hope of glory in Heaven.

⋖§ I T I S so easy to lose Christ; He can even be lost by a little heedlessness; a little want of watchfulness and the Divine Presence slips away. But sometimes a reconciliation is sweeter than an unbroken friendship. There are two ways of knowing how good God is: one is never to lose Him, the other is to lose Him and find Him again.

⋖§ M A N Y a cross we bear is of our own manufacture; we made it by our sins. But the Cross which the Saviour carried was not His, but ours. One beam in contradiction to another beam was the symbol of our will in contradiction to His own. To the pious women who met Him on the roadway, He said: "Weep not for Me." To shed tears for the dying Saviour is to lament the remedy; it were wiser to lament the sin that caused it. If Innocence itself took a Cross, then how shall we, who are guilty, complain against it?

⋖§ L O V E is not to be measured by the joys and pleasures which it gives, but by the ability to draw joy out of sorrow, a resurrection out of a crucifixion, and life out of death. Unless there is a Cross in our life, there will never be an empty tomb; unless there is the crown of thorns, there will never be the halo of light: "O, Death, where is thy victory? O, grave, where is thy sting?"

⋖§ E V E R Y P E R S O N has a destiny—a final destiny. He has lesser goals, too, such as making a living, rearing a family, but over and above all, there is his supreme goal, which is to be perfectly happy. This he can be if he has a life without end or pain or death, a truth without error or doubt, and an eternal ecstasy of love without satiety or loss. Now this Eternal Life, Universal Truth, and Heavenly Love is the definition of God. To refuse this final perfect end and to substitute a passing, incomplete, unsatisfying object, such as flesh or ambitious ego, is to create an inner unhappiness that no psychiatrist can heal!

✥ WHAT mysterious power is it that a mother has over a son that, when he confesses his guilt, she strives to minimize it, even when it shocks her heart at the perversity of the revelation? The impure are rarely tolerant of the pure, but only the pure can understand the impure. The more saintly the soul of a confessor, the less he dwells on the gravity of the offense, and the more on the love of the offender. Goodness always lifts the burden of conscience, and it never throws a stone to add to its weight. There are many sheaves in the field which the priests and sisters and the faithful are unable to gather in. It is Mary's role to follow these reapers to gather the sinners in. As Nathaniel Hawthorne said: "I have always envied the Catholics that sweet, sacred, Virgin Mother who stands between them and the Diety, intercepting somewhat His awful splendor, but permitting His love to stream on the worshipper more intelligibly to human comprehension through the medium of a woman's tenderness."

✥ BAD TEMPER is an indication of a man's character; every man can be judged by the things which make him mad. Heaven could be ruined by one single soul who was *touchy*.

✥ THROUGHOUT the Christian centuries those who were burdened with guilt and afraid to approach God, or who had not come to the Divinity of Christ, or who, having come, were so stricken with shame that they fell back into sadness, have had recourse to the Blessed Mother to lift them out of the abyss. Typical of this spirit are two modern

146

writers. W. T. Titterton, the poet and essayist, on the occasion of Shaw's death wrote: "Shaw was great friends with a Reverend Mother who prayed daily for his conversion. Once he confessed to her his difficulty: he could not believe in the Divinity of Christ. 'But,' he said, patting her shoulder, 'I think His Mother will see me through.'" Shaw put his finger on the sublime truth that those who are not yet ready to accept Christ as the mediator between God and man will come to that truth through Mary, who will act as the mediatrix between widowed souls and Christ, until they finally come to His embrace.

&§ NO SINNER in the world is beyond the hope of redemption; no one is so cursed that he cannot obtain pardon if he but calls on Mary. It is necessary to be in the state of sanctifying grace to be saved, but it is not necessary to be in the state of grace to call on Mary. As she was the representative of sinful humanity who gave consent to the Redemption, so she is still the representative of those who are not yet in the state of friendship with God. It is easy for the brothers of Christ to call on the Father, but it is not easy for the strangers and the enemies. This role Mary plays. She is not only the Mother of those who are in the state of grace, but the Queen of those who are not.

&§ THE sense of justice is so deep-rooted in us that if we are not good, we try to pacify our consciences by attributing the same evil to others. Charity, on the contrary, is unsuspicious; and, because it believes in others, is most encouraging of good. Charity never imputes the evil motive, never judges solely by externals.

&§ JUST as the waters of the sea reflect the light of the moon and mirror its glamour, so too does all visible creation reveal the attributes of God. And because no creature could possibly reflect all His perfections He multiplied and diversified creatures, so that what one lacks the other might supply.

147

Thus the totality of the universe, like a great orchestra made up of many instruments, proclaims His perfections more than any one creature, however perfect, could do. Every object which the mind can discern is a letter of the living Word of God. Some men, always children mentally, play with the alphabet blocks as so many meaningless toys, never dreaming to spell the word, until it is too late—when the universe is taken away. Others, there are, who see meaning in the blocks, and it is these who learn to read the sentence that stands first in the primer of life: God made the world.

⇥ THE Mass is an act, not a prayer recited. It is the immortal sacrifice of Christ renewed on our altars.

⇥ THE Sacraments are the communication of the life of God. First, we must be born: that is Baptism; second, we must grow spiritually and reach the stage of Christian virility: that is Confirmation; third, we must nourish our souls on the Bread of Life: that is the Eucharist; fourth, we must bind up our spiritual wounds: that is Penance; fifth, we must root out all traces of spiritual infirmities: that is Extreme Unction. But we are also social beings. We need government and a source of unity and the priesthood: that is Holy Orders. We need to continue the existence of the race: that is Matrimony.

⇥ THERE are seven ways in which Charity may be expressed physically:

> To feed the hungry.
> To give drink to the thirsty.
> To clothe the naked.
> To succor the stranger.
> To visit the sick.
> To ransom the captive.
> To bury the dead.

◈ As LONG AS the soul dominates the body, as long as man follows the dictates of right reason, man lives a moral existence naturally. But experience bears out what Revelation teaches, namely that man cannot keep the whole moral law over a long period of time without falling into sin. Man therefore needs help from above and aids which nature cannot supply, and this higher life which gives strength to the soul is grace. It makes us children of God, partakers of the Divine Nature, and heirs of heaven. Grace is the life of Christ in the soul. We said before that man lives naturally when the life of the soul dominates the life of the body: here we add that man lives supernaturally as long as the life of Christ dominates the soul and through it all nature. It is thanks to this participated life of God in the soul through grace that even the human body takes on a new dignity.

◈ As ALL CREATION revolves about man, so too, man revolves about Jesus Christ. Man is the pivot about which the whole order of nature swings; Jesus Christ is the pivot about which all supernature swings. This is the point to which we must ever recur, for without Christ this world of ours loses its intelligibility and meaning.

◈ FORTITUDE may be defined as that virtue which enables us to face undismayed and fearlessly the difficulties and dangers which stand in the way of duty and goodness. It stands midway between foolhardiness, which rushes into danger heedlessly, and cowardice, which flees from it recreantly. Because fortitude is related to bravery, it must not be thought that bravery is devoid of fear; rather it is control of fear. Fortitude is of two kinds, depending upon whether it is directed to a natural good or a supernatural good.

A soldier, for example, who braves the dangers of battle for love of country practices natural fortitude. But the saint who overcomes all difficulties and dangers for the sake of the glory of God and the salvation of his soul practices supernatural fortitude.

149

⊷§ THERE ARE many good men and women tossing on beds of pain, their bodies wasted by long sickness, their hearts broken with woe and sorrow, or their minds tortured by irreparable loss of friends and fortune. If these souls want peace they must recognize that in this world there is no intrinsic connection between personal sin and suffering.

⊷§ THE shock of sorrow comes only to those who think this world is fixed and absolute, that there is nothing beyond. They think everything here below should be perfect. Hence they ask questions: "Why should I suffer? What have I done to deserve this?" Maybe you did nothing to deserve it. Certainly Our Lord did nothing to deserve His Cross. But it came and through it He went to His glory.

The virtue to be cultivated then by such souls is what is known as Patience. Patience and Fortitude are related as the convex and concave sides of a saucer. Fortitude is exercised in the active struggle with dangers and difficulties, while Patience is the passive acceptance of what is hard to bear.

⊷§ TO TAKE the Cross God sends us as He took the one given to Him, even though we do not deserve it, is the shortest way to identification with God's will which is the beginning of Power and Peace: Power because we are one with Him who can do all things; Peace because we are tranquil in the love of Him who is just.

⊷§ MOST PEOPLE today want a religion which suits the way they live, rather than one which makes demands upon them. The result is that in order to make religion popular too many prophets have watered down religion until it is hardly distinct from sentimental secularism. Religion thus becomes a luxury like an opera, not a responsibility like life.

There is no doubt that a religion which makes concessions to human weakness will be popular; for example, one that denies hell for those who are unjust, and is silent about divorce for those who have repudiated their vows.

&§ THE *virtue* of Hope is quite different from the *emotion* of Hope. The emotion centers in the body and is a kind of dreamy desire that we can be saved without much effort. The virtue of Hope, however, is centered in the will and may be defined as a divinely infused disposition of the will by which with sure confidence, thanks to the powerful help of Almighty God, we expect to pursue eternal happiness, using all the means necessary for attaining it.

&§ IN A single moment a soul with a genuine fear of God can come to a greater understanding of the purpose of life than in a life-time spent in the study of the ephemeral philosophies of men. That is why death-bed conversions may be sincere conversions. The hardened soul disbelieves in God until that awful moment when he has no one to deceive but himself. Once the spark of salutary fear of God had jumped into the soul of the thief from the flaming furnace of that central Cross, fear gave way to faith. His next words were believing.

&§ YOU may sin a thousand times and be forgiven, but like the man who threw himself into a river a hundred times, each time to be rescued by the bridge-tender, you may be told by the rescuer: "Some day you will throw yourself into the river and I may not be here to pull you out."

R EGARDLESS however of how multi-
plied or grievous your sins may have been, there is still room
for hope. Did not Our Lord say: "For I came not to call the
just, but sinners" (MARK 2:17); and on another occasion "there
shall be joy in heaven upon one sinner that doth penance, more
than upon ninety-nine just who need not penance. (LUKE 15:7.)

If He forgave the thief, and Magdalene, and Peter, why not
you? What makes many in old age sad is not that their joys
are gone, but that their hopes are gone. Your earthly hopes may
decrease with the years, but not heavenly hope. Regardless of
the sinful burden of the years, God's mercy is greater than your
faults.

Only when God ceases to be infinitely merciful and only
when you begin to be infinitely evil, will there be reason for
despair; and that will be never; Peter denied Our Lord, but
Our Lord did not deny Peter. The thief cursed Christ, but He

did not curse the thief. If we had never sinned we could never call Christ Saviour.

✻ THERE ARE many falsehoods told about the Catholic Church: One of them is that Catholics adore Mary. This is absolutely untrue. Mary is a creature, human, not Divine. Catholics do not adore Mary. That would be idolatry. But they do reverence her.

✻ THE higher our loves and ideals, the nobler will be our character. The problem of character training is fundamentally the inculcation of proper ideals. That is why every nation holds up its national heroes, that citizens may become like to them in their patriotism and devotion to country.

If we have heroes and ideal protypes for those who love sports, the stage, country, army and navy, why should there not be an ideal in the all-important business of leading a good life and saving our souls?

That is precisely one of the roles the Blessed Mother of Our Divine Lord plays in Christian life: An object of love so pure, so holy, and so motherly that to be worthy of it we refrain from doing anything which might offend her.

✻ THE level of any civilization is the level of its womanhood. What they are, men will be, for, to repeat, love always goes out to meet the demands of the object loved. Given a woman like the Mother of Our Lord as our supernatural Mother, you have one of the greatest inspirations for nobler living this world has ever known.

✻ THERE IS told a legend which illustrates the intercessory power of Our Blessed Lady: It seems that one day Our Blessed Lord was walking through the Kingdom of Heaven and saw some souls who had got in very easily. Approaching Peter at the Golden Gate He said: "Peter, I have given to you the keys to the Kingdom of Heaven. You must use your power wisely and discreetly. Tell Me, Peter, how did these souls gain entry into My Kingdom?" To which Peter answered: "Don't blame me, Lord. Every time I close the door, Your Mother opens a window."

✻ WHEN anyone asks us to join the Church he is not immediately accepted. He must first undergo instructions of between forty and one hundred hours extending over several months. Converts are not first told: "You must believe everything the Catholic Church teaches" but rather, "You must have a reason for believing its teachings." Absolutely nothing is taken for granted. We do not say: "We will start with God." No! We start with the world. Using reason we first prove the existence of God and His nature.

Enquiry precedes conviction. Enquiry is a matter for reason which weighs the evidence and says: "I ought to believe." But submission is an act of the will. It is at this point many fail, either because too absorbed by the pleasures of the world, or because fearful of the scorn of others.

✻ A CATHOLIC may be defined as one who made the startling discovery that God knows more than he does.

✻ THE only times some people think of God is when they are in trouble, or when their pocketbook is empty, or they have a chance to make it a little fatter. They flatter themselves that at such moments they have faith when really they have only earthly hope for good luck.

It cannot be repeated too often: faith bears on the soul and its salvation in God, not on the baubles of earth.

✻ WE DO RECOGNIZE that with Protestants and Jews we have God, morality and religion in common. In the name of God, let us, Jews, Protestants and Catholics, do two things: (1) Realize that an attack upon one is an attack upon all, since we are all one in God; it is not Tolerance we need, but Charity; not forbearance but love.

(2) Begin doing something about religion, and the least we can do is to say our prayers: to implore God's blessings upon the world and our country; to thank Him for His blessings; and to become illumined in the fullness of His truth.

✱ TEMPERANCE must not be confused with Puritanism, which because of the abuse of a thing would take away its use; nor with license which would interpret all restraint as an infringement of liberty. Rather, there is a golden mean, as revealed in Our Lord's first miracle at Cana where he changed water into wine to satisfy the individual appetite and blessed the married couple for the satisfaction of the creative instinct.

✱ A SAINT is always joyful, but our modern pleasure-hunter is always melancholy. He is not really happy, because he laughs too much. His laughter is artificially stimulated from the outside by a stooge with a wise-crack; it is not a joy that proceeds from the inside because of a duty fulfilled out of love of God. Happiness comes from self-possession through temperance, not from self-expression through license.

✱ THERE IS a story told of a woman who gave a fortune motivated by human glory, and very occasionally a meager gift for a spiritual intention. When she went to heaven St. Peter showed her a tiny insignificant little house, which was dwarfed by all the mansions surrounding it. "I cannot live in that," said the woman. St. Peter answered: "Sorry, lady. That was the best I could do with the materials you sent me."

✱ FOR those who wish to cultivate the virtue of temperance and to be self-possessed, these two specific recommendations are made: First, each day practice at least three trivial mortifications, for example, giving up the ninth cigarette, holding back the sarcastic word, returning a kindly answer to a sneer, or sealing the lips on the scandal you just heard, which probably, like all scandals, is 99 44/100 per cent untrue.

Second, the magnitude of the mortification is not as important as the love of God for which it is done. Great sacrifices without love are worthless for the soul; nor because they are great does it follow they were done with love; it is the motive that matters—do them out of love of God.

❋ T H E most degraded man on the face of the earth is precious, and Christ died for Him. That poor soul may have made the wrong choice, but that is not for us to decide. While he has life, he has hope. He might not seem lovable to us, but he is loved by God.

❋ L o v e wills not to keep the secrets of His Wisdom to Himself but tells them to man—and this is Revelation.

Love tends to become like the one loved, and since God loved man, God became man—and this is the Person of Jesus Christ, true God and true man.

Love seeks to take another's pain and sin as its own and thus to make it whole—and this was the Cross and Redemption.

Love seeks not only to give what it has, but even to communicate its very Spirit—and this was Pentecost and the Birthday of the Church.

❋ T h e *Love of God is Freedom!*
How could love be love if it were forced? By making man free, God made it possible for man to reject Divine Love. Man cannot be made to love God any more than he can be made to enjoy Bach's classical music. The power of choice is not necessarily the choice of what is best. Hence, "If you love me, keep my commandments." (John 14:15.)

✳ THERE ARE only two things that could possibly remove evil and suffering from the world: either the conformity of human wills to the will of God, or God becoming a dictator and destroying all human wills.

Why is it that men, who by forgetting the Love of God turn the universe into a house of mass-suicide, never think of blaming themselves, but immediately put God on the judgment seat, and question His Love and Goodness?

We all have a share in the evils of the world, and it ill behooves us to ignore our faults and become critics of God. It is we who are in the prisoners' dock in a world crisis like this. Instead of questioning the God of Love, we ought to be throwing ourselves on the Mercy of His Judgment.

✳ THESE are several ways to avoid loving God:

Deny that you are a sinner.

Pretend that religion is for the ignorant and the superstitious, but not for the truly learned such as yourself.

Insist that the sole purpose of religion is social service.

Judge religion by whether or not it is accepted by the "important" people of the world.

Avoid all contemplation, self-examination and inquiry into the moral state of your soul.

Take yourself very seriously.

✳ AN ANIMAL seeks pleasure within the finite limits of his physical organism; but man wants it to satisfy the infinite thirst of his soul. In man, therefore, the law of diminishing returns operates: As pleasure decreases, the desire for it increases. Pleasures then begin to exasperate because they "lie"; they do not give what they promised. Sadness, bitterness and cynicism sometimes seize the soul, and with it a fatigue of life. That very emptiness can be the foundation of conversion. The desire for happiness could not be wrong. It must be, therefore, that we sought happiness in the wrong objects: in creatures apart from God, instead of in creatures under God's law. Thus, in the very confusion and disgust following sin is hidden a sense of awakened spiritual possibilities. A soul is on the verge of knowing itself when it knows that acting like a beast it *might* live like an angel. After having fed himself on husks, the prodigal began to yearn for the bread of the father's house.

✶ MANY PERSONS identify themselves with their environment. Because life is good to them, they believe they are good. They never dwell on eternity because time is so pleasant. When suffering strikes, they become divorced from their pleasant surroundings and are left naked in their own souls. They then see that they were not really affable and genial, but irritable and impatient. When the sun of outer prosperity sank, they had no inner light to guide their darkened souls. It is, therefore, not what happens to us that matters; it is how we react to it.

No one is better because of pain; conceivably a man may become seared and scarred by pain. But, the very emptiness of soul that follows enforced divorce from pleasurable surroundings does drive the soul back unto itself, and if it cooperates with grace at that moment, it may find the meaning of life. It was through a wound that St. Ignatius came to know himself. Many in life do not meet Christ until, like the thief on the right, they find Him on a Cross. On the battlefields in war many a man has found Him the only One to whom to turn.

✶ SOMETIMES it has happened that a man who had never given a thought to religion entered a Catholic Church and although he knew nothing of her teaching, after half an hour or more spent in the presence of the Blessed Sacrament, was seized with a sense that "Something or Someone is there" that makes the church different. Such a soul does not know or believe that Our Lord is really and truly present on the altar of every Catholic Church. He does know that he feels "impelled" to remain in that mysterious Presence. Like the disciples of Emmaus, the soul has been companioning with the Saviour without knowing it.

✳ WHY do we love to see, on the stage or screen, doleful and tragical things which we never would want to befall us? Why should sorrow be our pleasure and tears be our satisfaction? Why do we weep for the fanciful on the stage, but not for the reality? Why do we, who would have none of our friends murdered, love to read about murders? Do men who are at peace want to see feigned misery? Do those who are glad rejoice in pretended tragedy?

Is not our desire to see that which is sad or tragic a revelation of the sadness and tragedy of our own souls? A soul that loves God and sees misery wants to relieve it; a soul that has abandoned God and sees misery wants to weep over it, not knowing that he is really weeping over himself. We act as mourners when we really are the mourned.

The moment we realize that our sadness is born of our sins, we are ripe for conversion. Then we feel the poignancy of the invitation: "Come to me, all you that labour, and are burdened, and I will refresh you." (MATTHEW 11:28.)

✳ WHAT *is a sacrament?* In the broad sense a sacrament is a material, visible thing used as a channel for the spiritual and the invisible. The world is made up of sacraments of the natural order. A handshake is a sacrament, in the sense that it is a visible clasping of hands to express the invisible; namely, welcome and friendship.

✳ WHY *is sin wrong?* Because sin is a divorce of man from the Divine Life in the soul. What death is to the body, that sin is to the soul. "For the wages of sin is death." (ROMANS 6:23.) Man in the state of grace has a double "life." The life of the body is the soul; the life of the soul is grace. When the soul leaves the body, the body dies. When grace leaves the soul, the soul dies. This is a "double death." That is why the greatest tragedy in the world is to die in the state of sin.

✳ A T W H A T M O M E N T do Catholics render most glory to God? In the Holy Sacrifice of the Mass. For no man can glorify God as He deserves, except Our Lord because He is the Son of God and the Son of Man. Therefore, He is the Mediator between God and man. The only true worship of God is through Christ, and it is in the Mass that Jesus Christ is offered to the Father—but not Jesus Christ alone. We are with Him. The work of the Saviour is sufficient only for him who completes it on his own account. In the Mass we unite ourselves to the offering Christ made of Himself upon the Cross. When He died on the Cross we died with Him. "For the charity of Christ presseth us; judging this, that if one died for all, then all were dead." (II CORINTHIANS 5:14.)

✳ E N V Y is discontent with another's good, a mentality which is cast down at another's good, as if it were an affront to our own superiority.

Do I assert my envy by "running down" others by innuendo, half-truths, fault-finding, or by attributing to them false motives?

Have I rejoiced over the misfortunes of others?

Have I ever tried to cure my jealousy by praying for the one of whom I was jealous?

Why have I not made the quality of a neighbor an occasion for imitation rather than envy, and thus increased in some way the welfare of humanity and the glory of God: "But if you bite and devour one another: take heed you be not consumed one of another." (GALATIANS 5:15.)

✳ U N J U S T A N G E R is a violent and inordinate desire to punish others, and is often accompanied by hatred which seeks not only to repel aggression, but to take revenge.

Am I impatient with others? Do I fly into "fits of temper" and make cutting and sarcastic remarks because my will has been crossed?

Do I ever practice patience, that is, think before I speak, then talk to myself?

Have I ever asked myself how will God forgive my sins if I do not forgive the faults of others?

Do I realize that being quickly aroused to anger is a sign of selfishness, and that my character is known from the things I hate? If I love God, I will hate sin; if I love sin, I will hate religion. "Judge not that you may not be judged." (MATTHEW 7:1.)

✴ GLUTTONY is the abuse of the lawful pleasure God has attached to eating and drinking, which are necessary conditions of self-preservation. It becomes sinful when it incapacitates us for the fulfillment of our duties, injures our health, endangers the interests of others, or when—for Catholics —it breaks the laws of fast and abstinence.

✴ SLOTH is a malady of the will which causes us to neglect our duties. It is physical sloth when it manifests itself in laziness, procrastination, idleness and indifference. It is spiritual sloth when it shows a distaste for the things of the spirit, a hurrying of devotions, a religious lukewarmness and a failure to cultivate new virtues.

✴ SELF-DISCIPLINE may be defined as a struggle against evil inclinations in order to subject them to our own will and ultimately to the will of God.

The modern world is opposed to self-discipline on the ground that personality must be "self-expressive." Self-expression is right so long as it does not end in self-destruction. A boiler that would be self-expressive by blowing up, or an engine that would be self-expressive by jumping the tracks, would both be acting contrary to their natures as fashioned by the minds of the engineers who designed them. So, too, if man acts contrary to what is best and highest in his nature by rebelling against the Eternal Reason of God, his Creator, his self-expression is self-destruction.

✳ THERE ARE two ways of coming to God: through the preservation of innocence; and through the loss of it. Some have come to God because they were good, like Mary, who was "full of grace"; like Joseph, the "just man"; like Nathaniel, "in whom there was no guile"; or like John the Baptist, "the greatest man ever born of woman."

But others have come to God who were bad, like the young man of the Gerasenes "possessed of devils," like Magdalene, out of whose corrupt soul the Lord cast seven devils; and like the thief at the right who spoke the second word to the Cross.

✳ IN THE face of that evil which is endemic in the human heart, this truth emerges: It is one thing to be blind and another thing to know it.

There is hope for those who are deaf and who want to hear and for the lame who want to walk, and there is hope for the diseased who acknowledges the need of a physician and the sinner who feels the need of a redeemer.

✳ OUR PRIDE makes us look down on people, so that we can never look up to God. In fact because our pride admits no law and no authority other than ourselves, it is essentially anti-God.

All our other sins can be from ourselves; for example, avarice, lust, anger, gluttony. But pride comes direct from hell. By that sin fell the angels. It destroys the very possibility of conversion.

If therefore we can humble ourselves as did the thief at the right, and admit we have done wrong, then out of our creative despair we can cry to the Lord to remember us in our misery! The very moment we stop strutting and posing and begin to see ourselves as we really are, then in our humility we shall be exalted.

✳ AS SOON AS we feel a great void in our souls, and realize that by our sinning we are no longer our own, and acknowledge that we are still thirsty at the border of a well, and admit that we have played the fool, and that our follies of the years mount up in their dark arrears, then out of a dark and swampy soul, we cry out with the thief—as all Catholics do when we go to confession—"Bless me Father, for I have sinned" —"I am a sinner."

Such is the beginning of salvation. The thief died a thief, for he stole Paradise. And if we win Paradise we will be thieves too, for we will never deserve what we got—the God of everlasting peace!

❋ CHRIST so loved us that He took our sins upon Himself as if He were guilty, and draws us freely to repentance by the price He paid to save us. Hence forgiveness is no glib thing! The Cross was the supreme expression of the righteousness of God!

If the redemption of man were done without cost, it would insult us, for no man with a sense of justice wants to be "let off." It would insult God, for the whole moral order founded on justice would be impugned. The Cross is the eternal proof that no sin is forgiven through indifference.

❋ THERE IS more possibility for conversion in a passion wrongly directed, than in indifference. Where there is fire, its direction can be changed by God's grace, so that it will burn upward rather than downward, and thus enkindle goodness rather than vice.

But where there is indifference and false tolerance and spineless broadmindedness that looks at all causes and espouses none —there is no chance.

❋ GOD walks into your soul with silent step. God comes to you, more than you go to Him. Every time a channel is made for Him, He pours into it His fresh gift of grace. And it is all done so undramatically—in prayer, in the sacraments, before the altar, in loving service of fellowman.

Never will His coming be what you expect, and yet never

will it disappoint. The more you respond to His gentle pressure, the greater will be your freedom.

✳ NO SOUL ever fell away from God without giving up prayer. Prayer is that which establishes contact with Divine Power and opens the invisible resources of heaven. However dark the way, when we pray, temptation can never master us.

✳ THE Church is totally indifferent to any regime. The Church adapts itself to all governments on condition that they respect liberty of conscience. It is indifferent as to whether people choose to live under a monarchy, republic, democracy or even a military dictatorship provided these governments grant the basic freedoms. If by "interference in politics" is meant the interference by the clergy in the political realm of the State, the Church is unalterably opposed to it, for the Church teaches that the State is supreme in the temporal order. But when politics ceases to be politics and begins to be a religion, when it claims supremacy over the soul of man, when it reduces him to a grape for the sake of the wine of collectivity, when it limits his destiny to be a servant of Moloch, when it denies both the freedom of conscience and freedom of religion, when it competes with religion on its own ground, the immortal soul that is destined for God, then religion protests. And when it does, its protest is not against politics but against a counter-religion that is anti-religious.

✳ EVERYONE in life has at least one great moment to come to God. How each of us reacts depends on whether we have a background of good will or bad will. In some there is a will to sin, occasional good actions being the interruptions to an abiding evil intention. In others there is a good will and though a bad action may occasionally cut a tangent across it, the will, being good, is ready to make amends and make all sacrifices to follow the directives of conscience and the actual graces of the moment.

✳ THE majority is not always right. Majority is right in the field of the relative, but not in the absolute. Majority is a legitimate test so long as voting is based on conscience and not on propaganda. Truth does not win when numbers qua numbers become decisive. Numbers alone can decide a beauty queen but not Justice. Beauty is a matter of taste, but Justice is tasteless. Right is still right if nobody is right, and wrong is still wrong if everybody is wrong. The first Poll in the history of Christianity was wrong!

✳ AN ESCAPIST is one who calls religion "escapism" so as to avoid that amendment of life which religion requires. His favorite expression is: "My conscience is at peace." But it is of a self-made and deceptive conscience that he speaks. A true conscience is not of our making; otherwise we could induce it always to testify in our defense, as alienists may sometimes testify in court for any side that hires them. Conscience cannot come to us from the rulings of society; otherwise it would never reprove us when society approves us, nor console us when society condemns. But a sound conscience stands firm, no matter whether we dislike its findings, and no matter whether those around us are opposed to them or not. Just as there is no way of knowing which keys on the piano ought to be played and which keys ought not be played, except by having a musical score outside the keys, so the very existence of conscience implies that there is outside of us a Divine Lawmaker, Who legislates—a Divine Executive, Who witnesses our correspondence with the law—and a Divine Judge, Who passes sentences. . . . The very word conscience means knowing with —knowing with Whom but God? For conscience is the impact of Divine Truth and Goodness on our inner self.

✳ HATRED is only love upside down.

✳ SUICIDE sometimes becomes the last resort of those who boast of an easy conscience; the disorder of a nature turned topsy-turvy—with the body subjugating the soul—seems no longer endurable. It is a psychological fact that a sense of something amiss within him makes a person strike his breast, whenever he has done wrong. The faithful do it three times when they recite the words of the Confiteor, "through my fault, through my fault, through my most grievous fault." It is as if there were something evil inside us that we should like to beat and to subdue. The executioners on Calvary left the hill striking their breasts, as if to drive out their crime. When deep despair settles on a sinful soul which has no outlet—either because it denies God or because it refuses to have recourse to His mercy—then this desire for self-infliction may reach a point where one takes his own life, as Judas did. The Judge had not yet appeared, and yet judgment had already judged: the elaborate and beautiful composite of body and soul was so disordered that the conscience now condemned it to be severed.

The sense of guilt is never completely destroyed in anyone. Conscience lives on, even when deliberately strangled or ignored.

NOTHING worth while is ever accomplished without passion—and the basic passion of all is love.

◈ SOME SOULS try to escape the reproaches of conscience by an excessive activity, even to the point of jitters and neurotic overwork. Happy people work, sometimes very hard, in the fulfillment of their duties. But others use work as a drug to keep their thoughts off their own conscience, their inner misery. When work is done for its own delight or to provide the economic necessities, it is normal; but when it is a compulsive escape from inner guilt, it ceases to be work and becomes an addiction. Normal work takes a man outside of himself, exteriorizes his ego, unites him with reality, and atones for his sins. But abnormal activity is one of the means a fearful ego uses in the effort to lose itself.

⋘ GOD loves us too much to leave us comfortable in our sins. Because the violinist wants the best from his violin, he tightens its strings in penitential disciplines, until they can give forth the perfect note; if endowed with consciousness, the violin would probably protest the sacrifice it had to make in preparation for the perfection it was destined to attain. We are like the violin.

⋘ SELF-MADE rationalizations always justify the egotist's flight from Goodness—as St. Augustine said: "I want to be chaste, dear Lord, a little later on. Not now!" The price of goodness frightened him. And when Our Divine Lord told St. Catherine of Siena that His Goodness chastened and purified souls, she said: "And that is why you haven't any friends." A rich ruler one day came to Our Lord and asked: "Master, who art so good, what must I do to win eternal life?" He was hoping for a pat answer, a less exigent formula for living, such as a merely human man might give him. Our Lord answered: "Why dost thou call Me good? None is good, except God only." In other words, "My Goodness is Divine Goodness. You will have to derive your own goodness from that Source, too." When Our Lord told him to sell all he had and follow Him, the Gospel says, "The answer filled him with sadness, for he was very rich." (LUKE 18:15.) Goodness demands that we be perfect, and nothing less will ever satisfy God. The thought of how much change in us this will require is always frightening. We dread the pain more than we want the cure that it will bring.

⋘ IF AN EGOTIST really understood the psychology of the human mind, he would never be heard to say that God is wrathful—for such a statement publishes his sinfulness. As a brown-colored glass can make the water in it seem brown, although it is not, so the Love that waits for us, passing through our sinful lives, may seem like wrath and anger. A change in our behavior removes all the unhealthy fear of God.

⚜ LIFE is difficult for most of us because we have not read God's meaning, written in His universe. He gives us the power to have, and He promises us happiness through the right use of creatures. He intends that each thing be used as a sacrament, a channel, a steppingstone to Him—a reminder of how much He is to be loved. Every fine human love He meant us to take as a foretaste of Infinite Love, and if the human heart thrills us, so much more should the Divine Heart set us aflame. God gives us little snatches of His goodness in creatures, that we might want the Whole.

⚜ THE condition of having a good time is that one shall not be always trying to have a good time. There is no fun in life, if everything is funny; there is no pleasure in shooting firecrackers, if every day is the Fourth of July. Many people miss pleasure because they seek nothing else, so removing the first condition of enjoyment, which is contrast. In the liturgy of the Church, there is a constant contrast between joy and sacrifice, between fast and feast. Even during the seasons of Lent and Advent, when there is penance and pain, the Church inserts a Laetare and a Gaudete Sunday, on which we are called to rejoice. She does this, first of all, to remind people that penance is not perpetual; and, secondly, to prevent them from getting into a psychological rut.

⚜ THE pursuit of pleasure is a token of man's higher nature, a symptom of his loneliness in this world. Torn between what he has, which surfeits him, and the far-off Transcendent, which attracts him, every worldly man stands in grave danger of self-hatred and despair until he finds his true Infinite in God. As Pascal put it: "The knowledge of God without a perception of man's misery causes pride, and the knowledge of man's misery without a perception of God causes despair. Knowledge of Jesus Christ constitutes the middle course, because in Him we find both God and your own misery."

&§ THE proper attitude toward life is not one of pleasure seeking, but the cultivation of a Divine sense of humor within our human limitations. And what is humor? It is said that one has a sense of humor if he can "see the point" and that he lacks a sense of humor if "he cannot see the point." But God has made the world in such a way that He is the point of everything we see. The material is meant to be a revelation of the spiritual; the human, a revelation of the Divine; and the fleeting experiences of our days, a revelation of Eternity. The universe, according to God's original plan, was made transparent, like a windowpane: a mountain was not to be just a mountain, but a symbol of the power of God. A snowflake was not just a snowflake, but a clue to the purity of God. Everything created was to tell something about God, for "by the visible things of the world is the Invisible God made manifest." According to this plan, every man was to be a poet, a humorist, a man endowed with a sense of the invisible, infinite values in everything.

&§ NO CHARACTER or temperament is fixed. To say "I am what I am, and that I must always be," is to ignore freedom. Divine Action in the soul, and the reversibility of our lives can make them the opposite of what they are.

&§ ONLY those people who believe in transcendent reality can pass through this life with a sure sense of humor. The atheist, the agnostic, the sceptic, the materialist—all these have to take themselves seriously; they have no spiritual vantage point on which they can stand, look down upon themselves, and see how laughable they are. There is nothing more ludicrous than pretentiousness, and unless self-knowledge comes to puncture it, the absurdity will grow. Yet, if our self-exaltation is deflated without a recognition of the Mercy of God, Who can lift up the sinner, then it may beget despair: God is required for gaiety.

&§ MAN is the only creature in the visible universe who can know himself—can turn around and observe his own thoughts, as it were, in a mirror. A stone, a tree, an animal—such things cannot turn back in their thoughts to identify themselves, nor can they contemplate themselves or stand off and regard themselves as an object. But the human spirit can penetrate itself; it can be not only a subject but also the object of a thought; it can admire itself, be angry with itself, and even despair of itself. This capacity for self-reflection, which animals do not have, makes man superior to the animal but also makes him subject to mental disorders when the soul does not fulfill the high destiny to which it is called—when it refuses to use the human faculty of unprejudiced examination of the self and its acts. To surrender this activity is to move down from the human level to that of the animal; to replace the I with the ego; to enter into the realm of mental eccentricity.

◄§ T H E R E   I S a vast difference between the individual who gets drunk because he loves liquor and the one who does it because he hates or fears something else so much that he has to run away from it. The first becomes the drunkard, the second the alcoholic. The drunkard pursues the exhilaration of liquor; the alcoholic pursues the obliteration of memory. Very few women ever become alcoholics because they like alcohol; they become alcoholics because they violently dislike something else. That is why, in some instances, the cure of alcoholism implies the facing of the very problem one is seeking to escape. And this procedure is impossible without self-knowledge.

◄§ P R A Y E R is the lifting up of our hearts and minds to God. More simply still, it is communion with God.

◄§ S E L F - K N O W L E D G E demands the discovery of our predominant fault—of the particular defect which tends to prevail in us, affecting our sympathies, our decisions, desires, and passions. The predominant fault is not always clearly seen, because it acts as a Fifth Column in our souls. A man who by nature is gentle and kind may easily have his spiritual life ruined by the hidden fault of weakness toward ethical and moral issues. Another person, who by nature is courageous, may have as his predominant fault a bad temper—or fits of violence which he calls "courage." The existence of a predominant fault does not indicate that there is no good quality in us; yet our good qualities may possibly be rendered ineffective by this hidden defect. The quickest way to discover the predominant fault is to ask ourselves: "What do I think about most when alone? Where do my thoughts go when I let them go spontaneously? What makes me most unhappy when I do not have it? Most glad when I possess it? What fault irritates me most when I am accused of it, and which sin do I most vigorously deny possessing?"

⤗ E N V Y is sadness at another's good, as if that good were an affront to one's superiority. As the rich are avaricious, so the poor are sometimes envious. The envious person hates to see anyone else happy. The charm, the beauty, the knowledge, the peace, the wealth of others are all regarded as having been purloined from him. Envy induces ugly women to make nasty remarks about beautiful women, and makes the stupid malign the wise. Since the envious person cannot go up, he tries to achieve equality by pulling the other down. Envy is always a snob, is always jealous and possessive. To the envious, all who are polite are castigated as "high-hat"; the religious they dub "hypocrites"; the well-bred "put on airs"; the learned are "high-brow." Envy begins by asking, "Why shouldn't I have everything that others have?" and ends by saying, "It is because others have these virtues that I do not have them." Then envy becomes enmity; it is devoid of respect and honor, and, above all, it can never say, "Thank you," to anyone.

⤗ O N E of the most effective ways of counteracting jealousy and envy in ourselves is to say a prayer immediately for the intention of the person we resent. By referring our enemies to God and by spiritually wishing them well, we

174

crush the psychological impulse toward envy. A second means is to try to emulate those who provoke our envy: the Church holds up the good example of the Saints, not to depress us, but to impress us—not to discourage us in our failings, but to encourage us to greater efforts. "Let us keep one another in mind, always ready with incitements to charity and to acts of piety." (HEBREWS 10:24.)

  &s L u s t is not sex—for sex is purely biological and is a God-given capacity; nor is it love, which finds one of its lawful expressions in sex. Lust is the isolation of sex from true love. There is no passion which more quickly produces slavery than lust—as there is none whose perversions more quickly destroy the power of the intellect and the will. Excesses affect the reason in four ways: by perverting the understanding so that one becomes intellectually blind and unable to see the truth; by weakening prudence and a sense of values, thus producing rashness; by building up self-love to generate thoughtlessness; by weakening the will until the power of decision is lost and one becomes a prey to inconstancy of character.

  &s A n g e r is a violent desire to punish others. Here we refer not to righteous anger, such as that of Our Lord when He drove the buyers and sellers out of the Temple, but the wrong kind of anger, which expresses itself in temper, vindictiveness, tantrums, revenge, and the clenching of the fist. Anger's disguise in the egotist's eyes is the desire to "get even" or "not to let him get away with it." In the press and on the platform anger calls itself "righteous indignation"; but underneath, it is still a mania to exploit wrath, to malign, and to foment grievances. Anger is very common among those with bad consciences; thieves will become far angrier when accused of theft than any honest man; unfaithful spouses will fly into a rage when caught in infidelity; women guilty of jealousy and malice "take it out" on their employees in the home. Those who displease such egotists are repulsed violently, and the good who reproach them by the pattern of their virtue are viciously maligned.

◄§ GLUTTONY is an abuse of the lawful pleasure that God has attached to eating and drinking, which are a necessary means of self-preservation. It is an inordinate indulgence in the pleasures of eating and drinking, either by taking more than is necessary or by taking it at the wrong time or in too luxurious a manner. Gluttony disguises itself as "the good life," or as "the sophisticated way," or as "gracious living." An over-stuffed, double-chinned generation takes gluttony for granted, rarely considering it a sin.

◄§ SLOTH is a malady of the will which causes neglect of one's duty. In the physical realm it appears as laziness, softness, idleness, procrastination, nonchalance, and indifference; as a spiritual disease, it takes the forms of a distaste of the spiritual, lukewarmness at prayers, and contempt of self-discipline. Sloth is the sin of those who only look at picture-magazines, but never at print; who read only novels, but never a philosophy of life. Sloth disguises itself as tolerance and broadmindedness—it has not enough intellectual energy to discover Truth and follow it. Sloth loves nothing, hates nothing, hopes nothing, fears nothing, keeps alive because it sees nothing to die for. It rusts out rather than wears out; it would not render a service to any employer a minute after a whistle blows; and the more it increases in our midst, the more burdens it throws upon the State. Sloth is ego-centrical; it is basically an attempt to escape from social and spiritual responsibilities, in the expectation that someone else will care for us. The lazy man is a parasite. He demands that others cater to him and earn his bread for him; he is asking special privileges in wishing to eat bread which he has not earned.

◄§ ART is best known through its highest representative, not through those who daub.

◄§ Character grows by leaps and bounds as soon as one has ferreted out the master egotisms and removed the disguises of the superficial self. Self-knowledge is really the reversal of criticism from those around us to ourselves. Observing the neighbor's fault, the neighbor who before seemed hateful takes on a new lovableness. By losing our own pride and vanity, we gain a world of friends.

◄§ There are four wounds in human nature which make goodness an effort for us. One wound is in the intellect and reason, which is somewhat darkened by the Fall and arrives at truth only with an effort; another wound is in the will, which can now pursue the highest good only by resisting the appeal of the lower. The two other wounds are of the passions: one inclines us to do the easy thing; the other inclines us to avoid doing what is hard. This means that we are bound to have temptations to do what is wrong; but the temptations themselves are not sinful, unless our will yields to them. A person cannot help having a temptation toward lust, any more than he can prevent the rumbling of his stomach when he is hungry; but he can refuse to commit adultery in the first instance, or gluttony in the second. The one point to be kept in mind is that no amount of libido, or passion, no external force, and no inner prompting to sin can make the human action of man anything but free. We are never tempted beyond our strength. Every moral failure is ours alone, because our choices are our own.

◄§ Self-discipline does not mean self-contempt or destruction of personality, but it rather aims at self-expression in the highest sense of the term. . . . A man is not self-expressive when he satisfies his lusts like the beasts; he is "self-expressive" when he orders his passions according to reason and the promptings of the Holy Spirit.

⋘ As a wise and cautious traveler, looking ahead, avoids obstacles in his path, so does the man who is on the way to heaven deliberately avoid those things which interfere with the development of his character and union with God. Many a soul who once had faith and lost it, and many men who no longer have well-integrated personalities in the natural order, can trace their loss of peace of soul and peace of mind to evil companionship or to an environment which robbed them of their heritage. Sacred Scripture warns us that "he that loveth danger shall perish in it."

⋘ When the passions are regulated and tamed, are made subservient to virtue, they become like a horse with a bit in his mouth.

⋘ Everyone in the world is defeated in one area of life or another. Some fall away from their high ideals; others bemoan their failure to marry or, having married, lament because the state failed to realize all its hopes and promises; others experience a decline of virtue, a gradual slipping-away into mediocrity, or a slavery to vice; others are subjected to weariness, a failure of health, or economic ruin. All these disappointments are voiced in the mournful regret: "If I only had my life to live over again!" But it is of the utmost importance that, in facing our defeats and failures, we shall never yield to discouragement; for discouragement, from a spiritual point of view, is the result of wounded self-love and is therefore a form of pride.

⋘ Show love to others, and everyone seems lovable. The law of physics that every action has a contrary and equal reaction has its psychological counterpart. If we sow the seed of distrust in society, society always returns the harvest of distrust. The emotional reprises of others can be used as the mirror of our own interior dispositions.

BECAUSE the development of character requires constant vigilance, our occasional failures must not be mistaken for the desertion of God. Two attitudes are possible in sin—two attitudes can be taken toward our lapses into sin: we can fall down, and get up; or we can fall down, and stay there. The fact of having fallen once should not discourage us; because a child falls, it does not give up trying to walk. As sometimes the mother gives the most attention to the child who falls the most, so our failures can be used as a prayer that God be most attentive to us, because of our greater weaknesses.

No CHARACTER, regardless of the depths of its vice or its intemperance, is incapable of being transformed through the cooperation of Divine and human action into its opposite, of being lifted to the I-level and then to the Divine level. Drunkards, alcoholics, dope fiends, materialists, sceptics, sensualists, gluttons, thieves—all can make that area of life in which they are defeated, the area of their greatest victory.

MANY PEOPLE like to discuss religion, to argue about it, but as if it were impersonal, as if they were discussing Indonesian ritual dances. They miss the many-splendored thing because they never relate what they know to their own lives.

F AITH will answer the principal problems of
your life: Why? Whence? Whither? If you are without faith,
you are like a man who lost his memory and is locked in a dark
room waiting for memory to come back. There are a hundred
things you can do: scribble on the wall paper, cut your initials
on the floor and paint the ceiling. But if you are ever to find
out why you are there, and where you are going, you will have
to enlarge your world beyond space and time. There is a door
out of that room. Your reason can find it. But your reason cannot create the light that floods the room, nor the new world in
which you move, which is full of signs on the roadway to the
City of Peace and Eternal Beatitude with God.

❋ H A V E Y O U noticed that as men lose faith in
God, they become selfish, immoral and cruel? On a cosmic scale,
as religion decreases, tyranny increases; as men lose faith in Di-

vinity, they lose faith in humanity. Where God is outlawed, there man is subjugated.

✻ I T I S not so much what happens in life that matters; it is rather how we react to it. You can always tell the character of a person by the size of the things that make him mad. Because modern man lives in a world which has reference to nothing but itself, it follows that when depression, war and death enter into his two-dimensional world he tumbles into the most hopeless despair.

A man can work joyfully at a picture puzzle, so long as he believes the puzzle can be put together into a composite whole. But if the puzzle is a hoax, or if it was not made by a rational mind, then one would go mad trying to work it out. It is this absence of purpose in life which has produced the fear and frustration of the modern mind.

✻ E V E R Y T H I N G that happens has been foreseen and known by God from all eternity, and is either willed by Him, or at least permitted.

God's knowledge does not grow as ours does, from ignorance to wisdom. The Fall did not catch God napping. God is Science, but He is not a scientist. God knows all, but He learns nothing from experience. He does not look down on you from Heaven as you look down on an ant-hill, seeing you going in and out of your house, walking to work, and then telling an angel-secretary to record the unkind word you said to the grocer-boy.

Why is it we always think of God as watching the bad things we do, and never the good deeds? God does not keep a record of your deeds. You do your own bookkeeping. Your conscience takes your own dictation. God knows all things merely by looking into Himself, not by reading over your shoulder.

✻ D O N O T T H I N K that because God knows all that, therefore, He has predetermined you to Heaven and hell independently of your merits and irrespective of your freedom.

Remember that in God there is no future. God knows all, not in the succession of time, but in the "now standing still" of eternity, i.e., all at once. His knowledge that you shall act in a particular manner is not the immediate cause of your acting, any more than your knowledge that you are sitting down caused you to sit down, or prevents you from getting up, if you willed to do it.

✳ THE evil which God permits must not be judged by its immediate effects, but rather by its ultimate effects. When you go to a theatre, you do not walk out because you see a good man suffering in the first act. You give the dramatist credit for a plot. Why cannot you do that much with God?

✳ WHAT often holds an atheist back from being a believer in God, and a believer in God from accepting the Divinity of Christ, and a believer in the Divinity of Christ from embracing the Divinity of His Mystical Body, and a Catholic from shining forth the Truth and Charity of Christ in His life? It is not that these blessings challenge credulity, but that they challenge character. As Chesterton so well answered when it was objected that Christianity had been tried and found wanting: "Christianity has been found hard, but not tried." Those who say that Christianity is impractical mean that they refuse to put it into practice—because their habit patterns protest the change. God's sunlight is shining outside our windows—but what good will it do to debate about its beauty if we are not willing to clean the windows of our behavior and see it for ourselves? Few are ignorant of sunlight; many are afraid to let it enter their lives.

✳ IT IS a law of nature that no one ever gets his second wind until he has used up his first wind. So it is with knowledge. Only when we practice the moral truths which we already know will a deeper understanding of those truths and a fuller revelation come to us. Each new height the mind reveals must be captured by the will before greater heights come into view. Religion, then, is not just a subject of discussion; it is a subject for decision.

✻ G o d solicits each of us by a dialogue no other soul can hear. His action on the soul is always for us alone. He sends no circular letters, uses no party lines. God never deals with crowds as crowds—they could give Him only earthly glory —but what He wants is each soul's singular and secret fealty. He calls His sheep by name; He leaves the ninety-nine that are safe to find the one that is lost. On the Cross He addresses the thief in the second person singular: "This day, thou shalt be with Me in Paradise."

✻ S o m e object that, inasmuch as God's Will will always be done, it can make no difference whether we pray; this is like saying: "My friend will either get better or worse; what good will it do to send for a doctor and give him medicine?"

God will not do what we can very well do for ourselves; He will not make a harvest grow without our planting the seed. It is a conditional universe in which man lives—to bring about an effect we wish, we must proceed along the road to it through its cause. If a boy studies, he will know; if he strikes a match, it will ignite. In the spiritual order we have the words of Our Lord: "Ask, and the gift will come; seek, and you shall find; knock and the door shall be opened to you." (MATTHEW 7:7.) But there must be the preparation for God's help through the asking, and the seeking, and the knocking. Millions of favors are hanging from Heaven on silken cords—prayer is the sword that will cut them. "See where I stand at the door, knocking; if anyone listens to my voice and opens the door, I will come in to visit him, and take my supper with him, and he shall sup with me." (APOCALYPSE 3:20.)

✳ A LITTLE GIRL at Christmas once prayed for a thousand dolls. Her unbelieving father on Christmas Day said: "Well, God did not answer your prayers, did He?" And she answered: "Yes, He did. God said no." This was the humble acceptance of His Will of the truly faithful.

✳ MANY BLESSINGS and favors come to those individuals and families which put themselves wholeheartedly in the area of God's love—their lives are in sharp contrast to those who exclude themselves from that area of love. In the raising of a family, if the economic is made a primary concern and the Providence of God secondary, it is not to be expected that there will be the same showering of gifts and care on God's part as in a family where Providence comes first. The parents who trust God can tap a source of power and happiness which the other family does not make available. As human friends give us more in proportion as we trust them, and less in proportion to our mistrust, so it is with the Divine Friend. Those who make it possible for God to give more through their trust in Him receive more.

✳ IF GOD sometimes seems slow to answer our petitions, there are several possible reasons. One is that the delay is for the purpose of deepening our love and increasing our faith; the other is that God is urging us. God may defer for some time the granting of His gifts, that we might the more ardently pursue, not the gift but the Giver. Or we may be asking Him for something He wants us to learn we do not need.

✳ A HIGHER FORM of prayer than petition—and a potent remedy against the externalization of life—is meditation. Meditation is a little like a daydream or a reverie, but with two important differences: in meditation we do not think about the world or ourselves, but about God. And instead of using the imagination to build idle castles in Spain, we use the will to make resolutions that will draw us nearer to one of the Father's mansions. Meditation is a more advanced spiritual act than "saying prayers."

＊ THE Lord hears us more readily than we suspect; it is our listening to Him that needs to be improved. When people complain that their prayers are not heard by God, what often has happened is that they did not wait to hear His answer.

＊ GOD cannot seize our wills or force us to use our trials advantageously, but neither can the Devil. We are absolute dictators in deciding whether we wish to offer our will to God. And if we turn it over to Him without reservation, He will do great things in us. As a chisel in the hands of Michaelangelo can produce a better statue than a chisel in the hands of a child, so the human will becomes more effective when it has become a liege of God than if we try to rule alone. Our wills operating under our own power may be busy about many things, but in the end they come to nothing. Under Divine Power, the nothingness of our wills becomes effective beyond our fondest dreams.

＊ THE things that happen to us are not always susceptible to our minds' comprehension or wills' conquering; but they are always within the capacity of our Faith to accept and of our wills' submission.

＊ THE difference between people who never get the breaks and those who make every Now an occasion for thanking God is this: the latter live in an area of love greater than their desire to "have their way." As a waif on the streets suffers misfortunes which the child in a loving family does not know, so the man who has not learned to place full trust in God suffers reverses and disasters which would not appear as troubles to loving souls. God does not show Himself equally to all creatures. He does show all men how to turn everything to joy.

This does not mean God is unfair, but only that it is impossible for even Him to show Himself to certain hearts under some conditions. The sunlight has no favorites, but it cannot shine as well on a dusty mirror as on a polished one. In the order of Divinity, there is nothing accidental; there is never a collision of blind forces, hurting us, at random. There is, instead, the meeting of a Divine Will and a human will which has a perfect trust that ultimate good is meant for it, although it may not understand how until eternity.

✳ MAN is distinguished from the animals by the possession of a rational soul which gives him his special human dignity. It is fitting that the principal effects of the infusion of Divine energy should be manifested in the two main faculties of the soul—the intellect and the will. Once the Divine Power penetrates the intellect, it becomes Faith; once It infuses the will, it becomes Hope and Charity. Thus are born the three great supernatural virtues, by which we can believe in God, and know Him, and love Him.

✳ FAITH is like a microscope, in that it enables us to perceive a deeper meaning in truths which we already know; it gives a new dimension of depth to our natural knowledge. Knowledge without Faith is often made up of bits of information, jumbled in a heap, like steel filings in a random pile; Faith, like a magnet, marshals them in order. Faith takes our uncorrelated facts and relates them to a single unity. Thanks to its illumination, the intellect now has a new solid frame for judging and estimating all the various segments of reality. The world is now seen from the Divine point of view, and through the Christ-mind.

✳ THE two greatest dramas of life are the soul in pursuit of God and God in pursuit of the soul. The first has less apparent urgency, for the soul that pursues God can do it leisurely, as Peter followed the Saviour from afar. But when God pursues the soul, He proves a Relentless Lover, Who will never leave the soul alone until He has won it or been conclusively denied.

DATE DUE

MR 15 '65			
JY 6 '65			
JY 20 '65			
AG 10 '65			
MR 7 '66			
JE 24 '66			
FE 23 '67			
MR 22 '67			
SE 13 '68			
AP 10 '69			
JY 3 '69			
JY 17 '69			
DE 12 '71			
MAR 14 1978			
GAYLORD			PRINTED IN U.S.A.